A Book of Scoundrels

Charles Whibley

Contents

A BOOK OF SCOUNDRELS

BY

Charles Whibley

INTRODUCTION

THERE are other manifestations of greatness than to relieve suffering or to wreck an empire. Julius Caesar and John Howard are not the only heroes who have smiled upon the world. In the supreme adaptation of means to an end there is a constant nobility, for neither ambition nor virtue is the essential of a perfect action. How shall you contemplate with indifference the career of an artist whom genius or good guidance has compelled to exercise his peculiar skill, to indulge his finer aptitudes? A masterly theft rises in its claim to respect high above the reprobation of the moralist. The scoundrel, once justice is quit of him, has a right to be appraised by his actions, not by their effect; and he dies secure in the knowledge that he is commonly more distinguished, if he be less loved, than his virtuous contemporaries.

While murder is well-nigh as old as life, property and the pocket invented theft, late-born among the arts. It was not until avarice had devised many a cunning trick for the protection of wealth, until civilisation had multiplied the forms of portable property, that thieving became a liberal and an elegant profession. True, in pastoral society, the lawless man was eager to lift cattle, to break down the barrier between robbery and warfare. But the contrast is as sharp between the savagery of the ancient reiver and the polished performance of Captain Hind as between the daub of the pavement and the perfection of Velasquez.

So long as the Gothic spirit governed Europe, expressing itself in useless ornament and wanton brutality, the more delicate crafts had no hope of exercise. Even the adventurer upon the road threatened his victim with a bludgeon, nor was it until the breath of the Renaissance had vivified the world that a gentleman and an artist could face the traveller with a courteous demand for his purse. But the age which witnessed the enterprise of Drake and the triumph of Shakespeare knew also the prowess of the highwayman and the dexterity of the cutpurse. Though the art displayed all the freshness and curiosity of the primitives, still it was art. With Gamaliel Ratsey, who demanded a scene from *Hamlet* of a rifled player, and who could not rob a Cambridge scholar without bidding him deliver an oration in a wood, theft was already better than a vulgar extortion. Moll Cutpurse, whose intelligence and audacity were never bettered, was among the bravest of the Elizabethans. Her temperament was as large and as reckless as Ben Jonson's own. Neither her tongue nor her courage knew the curb of modesty, and she was the first to reduce her craft to a set of wise and imperious rules. She it was who discovered the secret of discipline, and who insisted that every member of her gang should undertake no other enterprise than that for which nature had framed him. Thus she made easy the path for that other hero, of whom you are told that his band was made up "of several sorts of wicked artists, of whom he made several uses, according as he perceived which way every man's particular talent lay." This statesman—Thomas Dun was his name—drew up for the use of his comrades a stringent and stately code, while he was wont to deliver an address to all novices concerning the art and mystery of robbing upon the highway. Under auspices so brilliant, thievery could not but flourish, and when the Stuarts sat upon the throne it was already lifted above the level of questioning experiment.

Every art is shaped by its material, and with the variations of its material it must perforce vary. If the skill of the cutpurse compelled the invention of the pocket, it is certain that the rare difficulties of the pocket created the miraculous skill of those crafty fingers which were destined to empty it. And as increased obstacles are perfection's best incentive, a finer cunning grew out of the fresh precaution. History does not tell us who it was that discovered this new continent of roguery. Those there are who give the credit to the valiant Moll Cutpurse; but though the Roaring Girl had wit to conceive a thousand strange enterprises, she had not the hand to carry them out, and the first pickpocket must needs have been a man of action. Moreover, her nickname suggests the more ancient practice, and it is wiser to yield the credit to Simon Fletcher, whose praises are chanted by the early historians.

Now, Simon, says his biographer, was "looked upon to be the greatest artist of his age by all his contemporaries." The son of a baker in Rosemary Lane, he early deserted his father's oven for a life of adventure; and he claims to have been the first collector who, stealing the money, yet left the case. The new method was incomparably more subtle than the old: it afforded an opportunity of a hitherto unimagined delicacy; the wielders of the scissors were aghast at a skill which put their own clumsiness to shame, and which to a previous generation would have seemed the wildest fantasy. Yet so strong is habit, that even when the picking of pockets was a recognised industry, the superfluous scissors still survived, and many a rogue has hanged upon the Tree because he attempted with a vulgar implement such feats as his unaided forks had far more easily accomplished.

But, despite the innovation of Simon Fletcher, the highway was the glory of Elizabeth, the still greater glory of the Stuarts. "The Lacedæmonians were the only people," said Horace Walpole, "except the English who seem to have put robbery on a right foot." And the English of the seventeenth century need fear the rivalry of no Lacedæmonian. They were, indeed, the most valiant and graceful robbers that the world has ever known. The Civil War encouraged their profession, and, since many of them had fought for their king, a proper hatred of Cromwell sharpened their wits. They were scholars as well as gentlemen; they tempered their sport with a merry wit; their avarice alone surpassed their courtesy; and they robbed with so perfect a regard for the proprieties that it was only the prig and the parliamentarian who resented their interference.

Nor did their princely manner fail of its effect upon their victims. The middle of the seventeenth century was the golden age, not only of the robber, but of the robbed. The game was played upon either side with a scrupulous respect for a potent, if unwritten, law. Neither might nor right was permitted to control the issue. A gaily attired, superbly mounted highwayman would hold up a coach packed with armed men, and take a purse from each, though a vigorous remonstrance might have carried him to Tyburn. But the traveller knew his place: he did what was expected of him in the best of tempers. Who was he that he should yield in courtesy to the man in the vizard? As it was monstrous for the one to discharge his pistol, so the other could not resist without committing an outrage upon tradition. One wonders what had been the result if some mannerless reformer had declined his assailant's invitation and drawn his sword. Maybe the sensitive art might have died under this sharp rebuff. But none but regicides were known to resist, and their resistance was never more forcible than a volley of texts. Thus the High-toby-crack swaggered it with insolent gaiety, knowing no worse misery than the fear of the Tree, so long as he followed the rules of his craft. But let a touch of brutality disgrace his method, and he appealed in vain for sympathy or indulgence. The ruffian, for instance, of whom it is grimly recorded that he added a tie-wig to his booty, neither deserved nor received the smallest consideration. Delivered to justice, he speedily met the death his vulgarity merited, and the road was taught the salutary lesson that wigs were as sacred as trinkets hallowed by association.

With the eighteenth century the highway fell upon decline. No doubt in its silver age, the century's beginning, many a brilliant deed was done. Something of the old policy survived, and men of spirit still went upon the pad. But the breadth of the ancient style was speedily forgotten; and by the time the First George climbed to the throne, robbery was already a sordid trade. Neither side was conscious of its noble obligation. The vulgar audacity of a bullying thief was suitably answered by the ungracious, involuntary submission of the terrified traveller. From end to end of England you might hear the cry of "Stand and deliver." Yet how changed the accent! The beauty of gesture, the deference of carriage, the ready response to a legitimate demand—all the qualities of a dignified art were lost for ever. As its professors increased in number, the note of aristocracy, once dominant, was silenced. The meanest rogue, who could hire a horse, might cut a contemptible figure on Bagshot Heath, and feel no shame at robbing a poor man. Once—in that Augustan age, whose brightest ornament was Captain Hind—it was something of a distinction to be decently plundered. But a century later there was none so humble but he might be asked to empty his pocket. In brief, the blight of democracy was upon what should have remained a refined, secluded art y and nowise is the decay better illustrated than in the appreciation of bunglers, whose exploits were scarce worth a record.

James Maclaine, for instance, was the hero of his age. In a history of cowards he would deserve the first place, but the "Gentleman Highwayman," as he was pompously styled, enjoyed a triumph denied to many a victorious general. Lord Mountford led half White's to do him honour on the day of his arrest. On the first Sunday, which he spent in Newgate, three thousand jostled for entrance to his cell, and the poor devil fainted three times at the heat caused by the throng of his admirers. So long as his fate hung in the balance, Walpole could not take up his pen without a compliment to the man, who claimed to have robbed him near Hyde Park. Yet a more pitiful rascal never showed the white feather. Not once was he known to take a purse with his own hand, the summit of his achievement being to hold the horses' heads while his accomplice spoke with the passengers. A poltroon before his arrest, in Court he whimpered and whinnied for mercy, he was carried to the cart pallid and trembling, and not even his preposterous finery availed to hearten him at the gallows. Taxed with his timidity, he attempted to excuse himself on the inadmissible plea of moral rectitude. "I have as much personal courage in an honourable cause," he exclaimed in a passage of false dignity, "as any man in Britain; but as I knew I was committing acts of injustice, so I went to them half loth and half consenting; and in that sense I own I am a coward indeed."

The disingenuousness of this proclamation is as remarkable as its hypocrisy. Well might he brag of his courage in an honourable cause, when he knew that he could never be put to the test. But what palliation shall you find for a rogue with so little pride in his art, that he exercised it "half loth, half consenting"? It is not in this recreant spirit that masterpieces are achieved, and Maclaine had better have stayed in the far Highland parish, which bred him, than have attempted to cut a figure in the larger world of London. His famous encounter with Walpole should have covered him with disgrace, for it was ignoble at every point; yet the art was so little understood, that it merely added a leaf to his crown of glory. Now, though Walpole was far too well-bred to oppose the demand of an armed stranger, Maclaine, in defiance of his craft, discharged his pistol at an innocent head. True, he wrote a letter of apology, and insisted that, had the one pistol-shot proved fetal, he had another in reserve for himself. But not even Walpole would have believed him, had not an amiable faith given him an opportunity for the answering quip: "Can I do less than say I will be hanged if he is?"

As Machine was a coward and no thief, so also he was a snob and no gentleman. His boasted elegance was not more respectable than his art. Fine clothes are the embellishment of a true adventurer, but they hang ill on the sloping shoulders of a poltroon. And Maclaine, with all the ostensible weaknesses of his kind, would claim regard for the strength that he knew not. He occupied a costly apartment in St. James's Street; his morning dress was a crimson damask banjam, a silk shag waistcoat, trimmed with lace, black velvet breeches, white silk stockings, and yellow morocco slippers; but since his magnificence added no jot to his courage, it was rather mean than admirable. Indeed, his whole career was marred by the provincialism of his native manse. Yet he was the adored of an intelligent age, and he basked a few brief weeks in the noonday sun of fashion.

But distinction was not the heritage of the Eighteenth Century; its glory is that now and again a giant raised his head above the stature of a prevailing rectitude. The art of verse was lost in rhetoric; the noble prose, invented by the Elizabethans, and refined under the Stuarts, was whittled away to common sense by the admirers of Addison and Steele. Swift and Johnson, Gibbon and Fielding, were apparitions of strength in an amiable, ineffective age. They emerged sudden from the impeccable greyness, to which they afforded an heroic contrast. So, while the highway drifted—drifted to a vulgar incompetence, the craft was illumined by many a flash of unexpected genius. The brilliant achievements of Jonathan Wild and of Jack Sheppard might have relieved the gloom of the darkest era, and their separate masterpieces make some atonement for the environing cowardice and stupidity. Above all, the Eighteenth Century was Newgate's golden age; now for the first time and the last were the rules and customs of the Jug perfectly understood. If Jonathan the Great was unrivalled in the art of clapping his enemies into prison, if Jack the Slipstring was supreme in the rarer art of getting himself out, even the meanest criminal of his time knew what was expected of him, so long as he wandered within the walled yard, or listened to the ministrations of the snuff-besmirched Ordinary. He might show a lamentable lack of cleverness in carrying off his booty; he might prove a too easy victim to the wiles of the thief-catcher; but he never fell short of courage, when asked to sustain the consequences of his crime.

Newgate, compared by one eminent author to a university, by another to a ship, was a republic, whose liberty extended only so far as its iron door. But while there was no liberty without, there was license within; and if the culprit, who paid for the smallest indiscretion with his neck, understood the etiquette of the place, he spent his last weeks in an orgie of rollicking lawlessness. He drank, he ate, he diced; he received his friends, or chaffed the Ordinary; he attempted, through the well-paid cunning of the Clerk, to bribe the jury; and when every artifice had failed he went to Tyburn like a man. If he knew not how to live, at least he would show a resentful world how to die.

"In no country," wrote Sir T. Smith, a distinguished lawyer of the time, "do malefactors go to execution more intrepidly than in England;" and assuredly, buoyed up by custom and the approval of their fellows, Wild's victims made a brave show at the gallows. Nor was their bravery the result of a common callousness. They understood at once the humour and the delicacy of the situation. Though hitherto they had chaffed the Ordinary, they now listened to his exhortation with at least a semblance of respect; and though their last night upon earth might have been devoted to a joyous company, they did not withhold their ear from the Bellman's Chant. As twelve o'clock approached—their last midnight upon earth—they would interrupt the most spirited discourse, they would check the tour of the mellowest bottle to listen to the solemn doggerel. "All you that in the condemned hole do lie," groaned the Bellman of St. Sepulchre's in his duskiest voice, and they who held revel in the condemned hole prayed silence of their friends for the familiar cadences:

All you that in the condemn'd hole do lie, Prepare you, for to-morrow you shall die, Watch all and pray, the hour is drawing near, That you before th' Almighty must appear. Examine well yourselves, in time repent That you may not t' eternal flames be sent; And when St. Pulchre's bell to-morrow tolls, The Lord above have mercy on your souls. Past twelve o'clock !

Even if this warning voice struck a momentary terror into their offending souls, they were up betimes in the morning, eager to pay their final debt. Their journey from Newgate to Tyburn was a triumph, and their vanity was unabashed at the droning menaces of the Ordinary. At one point a chorus of maidens cast wreaths upon their way, or pinned nosegays in their coats, that they might not face the executioner unadorned. At the Crown Tavern they quaffed their last glass of ale, and told the landlord with many a leer and smirk that they would pay him on their way back. Though gravity was asked, it was not always given; but in the Eighteenth Century courage was seldom wanting. To the common citizen a violent death was (and is) the worst of horrors; to the ancient highwayman it was the odd trick lost in the game of life. And he endured the rope, as the practised gambler loses his estate, without blenching. One there was, who felt his leg tremble in his own despite: wherefore he stamped it upon the ground so violently, that in other circumstances he would have roared with pain, and he left the world without a tremor. In this spirit Cranmer burnt his recreant right hand, and in either case the glamour of a unique occasion was a stimulus to courage.

But not even this brilliant treatment of accessories availed to save the highway from disrepute; indeed, it had become the profitless pursuit of braggarts and loafers, long before the abolition of the stage-coach destroyed its opportunity. In the meantime, however, the pickpocket was master of his trade. His strategy was perfect, his sleight of hand as delicate as long, lithe fingers and nimble brains could make it. He had discarded for ever those clumsy instruments whose use had barred the progress of the Primitives. The breast-pocket behind the tightest buttoned coat presented no difficulty to his love of research, and he would penetrate the stoutest frieze or the lightest satin, as easily as Jack Sheppard made a hole through Newgate. His trick of robbery was so simple and yet so successful, that ever since it has remained a tradition. The collision, the victim's murmured apology, the hasty scuffle, the booty handed to the *aide-de-camp,* who is out of sight before the hue and cry can be raised—such was the policy advocated two hundred years ago; such is the policy pursued to-day by the few artists that remain.

Throughout the eighteenth century the art of cly-faking held its own, though its reputation paled in the glamour of the highway. It culminated in George Barrington, whose vivid genius persuaded him to work alone and to carry off his own booty; it still flourished (in a silver age) when the incomparable Haggart performed his prodigies of skill; even in our prosaic time some flashes of the ancient glory have been seen. Now and again circumstances have driven it into eclipse. When the facile sentiment of the Early Victorian Era poised the tear of sympathy upon every trembling eyelid, the most obdurate was forced to provide himself with a silk handkerchief of equal size and value. Now, a wipe is the easiest booty in the world, and the Artful Dodger might grow rich without the exercise of the smallest skill. But wipes dwindled, with dwindling sensibility; and once more the pickpocket was forced upon cleverness or extinction.

At the same time the more truculent trade of housebreaking was winning a lesser triumph of its own. Never, save in the hands of one or two distinguished practitioners, has this clumsy, brutal pursuit taken on the refinement of an art. Essentially modern, it has generally been pursued in the meanest spirit of gain. Deacon Brodie clung to it as to a diversion, but he was an amateur, without a clear understanding of his craft's possibilities. The sole monarch of housebreakers was

Charles Peace. At a single stride he surpassed his predecessors; nor has the greatest of his imitators been worthy to hand on the candle which he left at the gallows. For the rest, there is small distinction in breaking windows, wielding crowbars, and battering the brains of defenceless old gentlemen. And it is to such miserable tricks as this that he who two centuries since rode abroad in all the glory of the High-toby-splice descends in these days of avarice and stupidity. The legislators who decreed that henceforth the rope should be reserved for the ultimate crime of murder were inspired with a proper sense of humour and proportion. It would be ignoble to dignify that ugly enterprise of to-day, the cracking of suburban cribs, with the same punishment which was meted out to Claude Duval and the immortal Switcher. Better for the churl the disgrace of Portland than the chance of heroism and respect given at the Tree!

But where are the heroes whose art was as glorious as their intrepidity? One and all they have climbed the ascent of Tyburn. One and all, they have leaped resplendent from the cart. The world, which was the joyous playground of highwaymen and pickpockets, is now the Arcadia of swindlers. The man who once went forth to meet his equal on the road, now plunders the defenceless widow or the foolish clergyman from the security of an office. He has changed Black Bess for a brougham, his pistol for a cigar; a sleek chimney-pot sits upon the head, which once carried a jaunty hat, three-cornered; spats have replaced the tops of ancient times; and a heavy fur coat advertises at once the wealth and inaction of the modern brigand. No longer does he roam the heaths of Hounslow or Bagshot; no longer does he track the grazier to a country fair. Fearful of an encounter, he chooses for the fields of his enterprise the byways of the City, and the advertisement columns of the smugly Christian Press. He steals without risking his skin or losing his respectability. The suburb, wherein he brings up a blameless, flat-footed family, regards him as its most renowned benefactor. He is generally a pillar (or a buttress) of the Church, and oftentimes a mayor; with his ill-gotten wealth he promotes charities, and endows schools; his portrait is painted by a second-rate Academician, and hangs, until disaster overtakes him, in the town-hall of his adopted borough.

But how much worse is he than the High-toby-cracks of old! They were as brave as lions; he is a very louse for timidity. His conduct is meaner than the conduct of the most ruffianly burglar that ever worked a centre-bit. Of art he has not the remotest inkling: though his greed is bounded by the Bank of England, he understands not the elegancies of life; he cares not how he plumps his purse, so long as it be full; and if he were capable of conceiving a grand effect, he would willingly surrender it for a pocketed half-crown. This side the Channel, in brief, romance and the picturesque are dead; and in France, the last refuge of crime, there are already signs of decay. The Abbé Bruneau caught a whiff of style and invention from the past. That other Abbé—Rosselot was his name—shone forth a pure creator: he owed his prowess to the example of none. But in Paris crime is too often passionel, and a crime passionel is a crime with a purpose, which, like the novel with a purpose, is conceived by a dullard, and carried out for the gratification of the middle-class.

To whitewash the scoundrel is to put upon him the heaviest dishonour: a dishonour comparable only to the monstrously illogical treatment of the condemned. When once a hero has forfeited his right to comfort and freedom, when he is deemed no longer fit to live upon earth, the Prison Chaplain, encouraging him to a final act of hypocrisy, gives him a free pass (so to say) into another and more exclusive world. So, too, the moralist would test the thief by his own narrow standard, forgetting that all professions are not restrained by the same code. The road has its ordinances as well as the lecture-room; and if the thief is commonly a bad moralist, it is certain that no moralist was ever a great thief. Why then detract from a man's legitimate glory? Is it not wiser to respect "that deep intuition of oneness," which Coleridge says is "at the bottom of our faults as well as our virtues?" To recognise that a fault in an honest man is a virtue in a scoundrel? After all, he is eminent who, in obedience to his talent, does prodigies of valour unrivalled by his fellows. And none has so many opportunities of various eminence as the scoundrel.

The qualities which may profitably be applied to a cross life are uncommon and innumerable. It is not given to all men to be light-brained, light-limbed, light-fingered. A courage which shall face an enemy under the starlight, or beneath the shadow of a wall, which shall track its prey to a well-defended lair, is far rarer than a law-abiding cowardice. The recklessness that risks all for a present advantage is called genius, if a victorious general urge it to success; nor can you deny to the intrepid Highwayman, whose sudden resolution triumphs at an instant of peril, the possession of an admirable gift. But all heroes have not proved themselves excellent at all points. This one has been distinguished for the courtly manner of his attack, that other for a prescience which discovers booty behind a coach-door or within the pocket of a buttoned coat. If Cartouche was a master of strategy, Barring-ton was unmatched in another branch; and each may claim the credit due to a peculiar eminence. It is only thus that you may measure conflicting talents: as it were unfair to judge a poet by a brief experiment in prose, so it would be monstrous to cheapen the accomplishments of a pickpocket, because he bungled at the concealment of his gains.

But a stern test of artistry is the gallows. Perfect behaviour at an enforced and public scrutiny may properly be esteemed an effect of talent—an effect which has not too often been rehearsed. There is no reason why the Scoundrel, fairly beaten at the last point in the game, should not go to his death without swagger and without remorse. At least he might comfort himself with such phrases as "a dance without the music," and he has not often been lacking in courage. What he has missed is dignity: his pitfalls have been unctuosity, on the one side, bravado on the other. It was the Prison Ordinary who first misled him into the assumption of a piety which neither preacher nor disciple understood. It was the Prison Ordinary who persuad-ed him to sign his name to a lying confession of guilt, drawn up in accordance with a foolish and inexorable tradition, and to deliver such a last dying speech as would not disappoint the mob. The set phrases, the vain prayer offered for other sinners, the hypocritical profession of a superior righteousness, were neither noble nor sin-cere. When Tom Jones (for instance) was hanged, in 1702, after a prosperous ca-reer on Hounslow Heath, his biographer declared that he behaved with more than usual "modesty and decency," because he "delivered a pretty deal of good advice to the young men present, exhorting them to be industrious in their several callings." Whereas his biographer should have discovered that it is not thus that your true hero bids farewell to frolic and adventure.

As little in accordance with good taste was the last appearance of the infamous Jocelin Harwood, who was swung from the cart in 1692 for murder and robbery, He arrived at Tyburn insolently drunk. He blustered and ranted, until the spectators hissed their disapproval, and he died vehemently shouting that he would act the same murder again in the same case. Unworthy, also, was the last dying repartee of Samuel Shotland, a notorious bully of the Eighteenth Century. Taking off his shoes, he hurled them into the crowd, with a smirk of delight. "My father and mother often told me," he cried, "that I should die with my shoes on; but you may all see that I have made them both liars." A great man dies not with so mean a jest, and Tyburn was untouched to mirth by Shotland's facile humour.

On the other hand, there are those who have given a splendid example of a brave and dignified death. Brodie was a sorry bungler when at work, but a perfect artist at the gallows. The glory of his last achievement will never fade. The muttered prayer, unblemished by hypocrisy, the jest thrown at George Smith—a metaphor from the gaming-table—the silent adjustment of the cord which was to strangle him, these last offices were performed with an unparalleled quietude and restraint. Though he had pattered the flash to all his wretched accomplices, there was no trace of the last dying speech in his final utterances, and he set an example of a simple greatness, worthy to be followed even to the end of time. Such is the type, but others also have given proof of a serene temper. Tom Austin's masterpiece was in another kind, but it was none the less a masterpiece. At the very moment that the halter was being put about his neck, he was asked by the Chaplain what he had to say before he died. "Only," says he, "there's a woman yonder with some curds and whey, and I wish I could have a pennyworth of them before I am hanged, because I don't know when I shall see any again." There is a brave irrelevance in this very human desire, which is beyond praise.

Valiant also was the conduct of Roderick Audrey, who after a brief but brilliant career paid his last debt to the law in 1714. He was but sixteen, and, says his biographer, "he went very decent to the gallows, being in a white waistcoat, clean napkin, white gloves, and an orange in one hand." So well did he play his part, that one wonders Jack Ketch did not shrink from the performance of his. But throughout his short life, Roderick Audrey—the very name is an echo of romance!—displayed a contempt for whatever was common or ugly. Not only was his appearance at Tyburn a lesson in elegance, but he thieved, as none ever thieved before or since, with no other accomplice than a singing-bird. Thus he would play outside a house, wherein he espied a sideboard of plate, and at last, bidding his playmate flutter through an open window into the parlour, he would follow upon the excuse of recovery, and, once admitted, would carry off as much silver as he could conceal None other ever attempted so graceful an artifice, and yet Audrey's journey to Tyburn is even more memorable than the story of his gay accomplice.

But it is not only the truly great who have won for themselves an enduring reputation. There are men, not a few, esteemed, like the popular novelist, not for their art but for some foolish gift, some facile trick of notoriety, whose actions have tickled the fancy, not the understanding of the world. The coward and the impostor have been set upon a pedestal of glory either by accident or by the whim of posterity. For more than a century Dick Turpin has appeared not so much the greatest of highwaymen, as the Highwayman Incarnate. His prowess has been extolled in novels and upon the stage; his ride to York is still bepraised for a feat of miraculous courage and endurance; the death of Black Bess has drawn floods of tears down the most callous cheeks. And the truth is that Turpin was never a gentleman of the road at all! Black Bess is as pure an invention as the famous ride to York. The ruffian, who is said to have ridden the phantom mare from one end of England to the other, was a common butcher, who burned an old woman to death at Epping, and was very properly hanged at York for the stealing of a horse which he dared not bestride.

Not one incident in his career gives colour to the splendid myth which has been woven round his memory. Once he was in London, and he died at York. So much is true; but there is naught to prove that his progress from the one town to the other did not occupy a year. Nor is there any reason why the halo should have been set upon his head rather than upon another's. Strangest truth of all, none knows at what moment Dick Turpin first shone into glory. At any rate, there is a gap in the tradition, and the chap-books of the time may not be credited with this vulgar error. Perhaps it was the popular drama of Skelt which put the ruffian upon the black mare's back; but whatever the date of the invention, Turpin was a popular hero long before Ainsworth sent him rattling across England. And in order to equip this butcher with a false reputation, a valiant officer and gentleman was stripped of the credit due to a magnificent achievement. For though Turpin tramped to York at a journeyman's leisure, Nicks rode thither at a stretch—Nicks the intrepid and gallant, whom Charles II., in admiration of his feat, was wont to call Swiftnicks.

THE MYTH OF DICK TURPIN

This valiant collector, whom posterity has robbed for Turpin's embellishment, lived at the highest moment of his art. He knew by rote the lessons taught by Hind and Duval; he was a fearless rider and a courteous thief. Now, one morning at five of the clock, he robbed a gentleman near Barnet of £560, and riding straight for York, he appeared on the Bowling Green at six in the evening. Being presently recognised by his victim, he was apprehended, and at the trial which followed he pleaded a triumphant alibi. But vanity was too strong for discretion, and no sooner was Swiftnicks out of danger, than he boasted, as well he might, of his splendid courage. Forthwith he appeared a popular hero, obtained a commission in Lord Moncastle's regiment, and married a fortune. And then came Turpin to filch his glory! Nor need Turpin have stooped to a vicarious notoriety, for he possessed a certain rough, half-conscious humour, which was not despicable. He purchased a new fustian coat and a pair of pumps, in which to be hanged, and he hired five poor men at ten shillings the day, that his death might not go un-mourned. But, above all, he was distinguished in prison. A crowd thronged his cell to identify him, and one there was who offered to bet the keeper half a guinea that the prisoner was not Turpin; whereupon Turpin whispered the keeper, "Lay him the wager, you fool, and I will go you halves." Surely this impudent indifference might have kept green the memory of the man who never rode to York!

But if the Scoundrel may claim distinction on many grounds, his character is singularly uniform. To the anthropologist he might well appear the survival of a. savage race, and savage also are his manifold superstitions. He is a creature of times and seasons. He chooses the occasion of his deeds with as scrupulous a care as he examines his formidable crowbars and jemmies. At certain hours he would refrain from action, though every circumstance favoured his success: he would rather obey the restraining voice of a wise, unreasoning wizardry, than fill his pockets with the gold for which his human soul is ever hungry. There is no law of man he dares not break, but he shrinks in horror from the infringement of the unwritten rules of savagery. Though he might cut a throat in self-defence, he would never walk under a ladder; and if the 13th fell on a Friday, he would starve that day rather than obtain a loaf by the method he best understands. He consults the omens with as patient a. divination as the augurs of old; and so long as he carries an amulet in his pocket, though it be but a. pebble or a polished nut, he is filled with an irresistible courage. [FOOTNOTE *: See Leland's "Gypey Sorcery."] For him the worst terror of all is the evil eye, and he would rather be hanged by an unsuspected judge than receive an easy stretch from one whose glance he dared not face. And while the anthropologist claims him for a savage, whose civilisation has been arrested at brotherhood with the Solomon Islanders, the politician might pronounce him a true communist, in that he has preserved a wholesome contempt of property and civic life. The prig, again, would feel his bumps, prescribe a gentle course of bromide, and hope to cure all the sins of the world by a municipal Turkish bath. But the wise man, respecting his superstitions, is content to take him as he finds him, and to deduce his character from his very candid history, which is unaffected by prig or politician.

Before all things, he is sanguine; he believes that Chance, the great god of his endeavour, fights upon his side. Whatever is lacking to-day, to-morrow's enterprise will fulfil, and if only the omens be favourable, he fears neither detection nor the gallows. His courage proceeds from this sanguine temperament, strengthened by shame and tradition rather than from a self-controlled magnanimity; he hopes until despair is inevitable, and then walks firmly to the gallows, that no comrade may suspect the white feather. His ambition, too, is the ambition of the savage or of the child; he despises such immaterial advantages as power and influence, being perfectly content if he have a smart coat on his back and a bottle of wine at his elbow. He would rather pick a lock than batter a constitution, and the world would be well lost, so he and his doxy might survey the ruin in comfort.

But if his ambition be modest, his love of notoriety is boundless. He must be famous, his name must be in the mouths of men, he must be immortal (for a week) in a rough woodcut. And then, what matters it how soon the end? His braveries have been hawked in the street; his prowess has sold a Special Edition; he is the first of his race, until a luckier rival eclipses him. Thus, also, his dandyism is inevitable: it is not enough for him to cover his nakedness—he must dress; and though his taste is sometimes unbridled, it is never insignificant. Indeed, his biographers have recorded the expression of his fancy in coats and smallclothes as patiently and enthusiastically as they have applauded his courage. And truly the love of magnificence, which he shares with all artists, is sincere and characteristic. When an accomplice of Jonathan Wild's robbed Lady M n at Windsor, his equipage cost him forty pounds; and Nan Hereford was arrested for shoplifting at the very moment that four footmen awaited her return with an elegant sedan-chair.

His vanity makes him but a prudish lover, who desires to woo less than to be wooed; and at all times and through all moods he remains the primeval sentimentalist. He will detach his life entirely from the catchwords which pretend to govern his actions; he will sit and croon the most heartrending ditties in celebration of home-life and a mother's love, and then set forth incontinently upon a well-planned errand of plunder. For all his artistry, he lacks balance as flagrantly as a popular politician or an advanced journalist. Therefore it is the more remarkable that in one point he displays a certain caution: he boggles at a superfluous murder. For all his contempt of property, he still preserves a respect for life, and the least suspicion of unnecessary brutality sets not only the law but his own fellows against him. Like all men whose god is Opportunity, he is a reckless gambler; and, like all gamblers, he is monstrously extravagant. In brief, he is a tangle of picturesque qualities, which, until our own generation, was incapable of nothing save dulness.

The Bible and the Newgate Calendar —these twain were George Barrow's favourite reading, and all save the psychologist and the prig will applaud the preference. For the annals of the "family" are distinguished by an epic severity, a fearless directness of speech, which you will hardly match outside the **Iliad or the Chronicles of the Kings.** But the **Newgate Calendar** did not spring ready-made into being: it is the result of a curious and gradual development. The chap-books came first, with their bold type, their coarse paper, and their clumsy, characteristic woodcuts—the chap-books, which none can contemplate without an enchanted sentiment. Here at last you come upon a literature, which has been read to pieces. The very rarity of the slim, rough volumes, proves that they have been handed from one greedy reader to another, until the great libraries alone are rich enough to harbour them. They do not boast the careful elegance of a famous press: many of them came from the printing-office of a country town: yet the least has a simplicity and concision, which are unknown in this age of popular fiction. Even their lack of invention is admirable: as the same woodcut might be used to represent Guy, Earl of Warwick, or the last highwayman who suffered at Tyburn, so the same enterprise is ascribed with a delightful ingenuousness to all the heroes who rode abroad under the stars to fill their pockets.

The **Life and Death of Gamaliel Ratsey** delighted England in 1605, and was the example of after ages. The anecdote of the road was already crystallised, and henceforth the robber was unable to act contrary to the will of the chap-book. Thus there grew up a folklore of thievery: the very insistence upon the same motive suggests the fairy-tale, and, as in the legends of every country, there is an identical element which the pedants call "human"; so in the annals of adventure there is a set of invariable incidents, which are the essentials of thievery. The industrious hacks, to whom we owe the entertainment of the chap-books, being seedy parsons or lawyer's clerks, were conscious of their literary deficiencies: they preferred to obey tradition rather than to invent ineptitudes. So you may trace the same jest, the same intrigue through the unnumbered lives of three centuries. And if, being a philosopher, you neglect the obvious plagiarism, you may induce from these similarities a cunning theory concerning the uniformity of the human brain. But the easier explanation is, as always, the more satisfactory; and there is little doubt that in versatility the thief surpassed his historian.

Had the chap-books been still scattered in disregarded corners, they would have been unknown or misunderstood. But happily, a man of genius came in the nick to convert them into as vivid and sparkling a piece of literature as the time could show. This was Captain Alexander Smith, whose *Lives of the Highwaymen,* published in 1719, was properly described by its author as "the first impartial piece of this nature which ever appeared in English." Now, Captain Smith inherited from a nameless father no other patrimony than a fierce loyalty to the Stuarts, and the sanguine temperament which views in horror a well-ordered life. Though a mere foundling, he managed to acquire the rudiments, and he was not wholly unlettered when at eighteen he took to the road. His courage, fortified by an intimate knowledge of the great tradition, was rewarded by an immediate success, and he rapidly became the master of so much leisure as enabled him to pursue his studies with pleasure and distinction. When his companions damned him for a milksop, he was loftily contemptuous, conscious that it was not in intelligence alone that he was their superior. While the Stuarts were the gods of his idolatry, while the Regicides were the fiends of his frank abhorrence, it was from the Elizabethans that he caught the splendid vigour of his style; and he owed not only his historical sense, but his living English to the example of Philemon Holland. Moreover, it is to his constant glory that, living at a time that preferred as well to attenuate the English tongue as to degrade the profession of the highway, he not only rode abroad with a fearless courtesy, but handled his own language with the force and spirit of an earlier age.

He wrote with the authority of courage and experience. A hazardous career had driven envy and malice from his dauntless breast. Though he confesses a debt to certain "learned and eminent divines of the Church of England," he owed a greater debt to his own observation, and he knew—none better—how to recognise with enthusiasm those deeds of daring which only himself has rivalled. A master of etiquette, he distributed approval and censure with impartial hand; and he was quick to condemn the smallest infraction of an ancient law. Nor was he insensible to the dignity of history. The best models were always before him. With admirable zeal he studied the manner of such masters as Thucydides and Titus Livius of Padua. Above all, he realised the importance of setting appropriate speeches in the mouths of his characters; and, permitting his heroes to speak for themselves, he imparted to his work an irresistible air of reality and good faith. His style, always studied, was neither too low nor too high for his subject. An ill-balanced sentence was as hateful to him as a foul thrust or a stolen advantage.

Abroad a craftsman, he carried into the closet the skill and energy which distinguished him when the moon was on the heath. Though not born to the arts of peace, he was determined to prove his respect for letters, and his masterpiece is no less pompous in manner than it is estimable in tone and sound in reflection. He handled slang as one who knew its limits and possibilities, employing it not for the sake of eccentricity, but to give the proper colour and sparkle to his page; indeed, his intimate acquaintance with the vagabonds of speech enabled him to compile a dictionary of Pedlar's French, which has been pilfered by a whole battalion of imitators. Moreover, there was none of the proverbs of the pavement, those first cousins of slang, that escaped him; and he assumed all the license of the gentleman-collector in the treatment of his love-passages.

Captain Smith took the justest view of his subject. For him robbery, in the street as on the highway, was the finest of the arts, and he always revered it for its own sake rather than for vulgar profit. Though, to deceive the public, he abhorred villainy in word, he never concealed his admiration in deed of a "highwayman who robs like a gentleman." "There is a beauty in all the works of nature," he observes in one of his wittiest exordia, u which we are unable to define, though all the world is convinced of its existence: so in every action and station of life there is a grace to be attained, which will make a man pleasing to all about him and serene in his own mind." Some there are, he continues, who have placed "this beauty in vice itself; otherwise it is hardly probable that they could commit so many irregularities with a strong gust and an appearance of satisfaction." Notwithstanding that the word a "vice" is used in its conventional sense, we have here the key to Captain Smith's position. He judged his heroes' achievements with the intelligent impartiality of a connoisseur, and he permitted no other prejudice than an unfailing loyalty to interrupt his opinion.

Though he loved good English as he loved good wine, he was never so happy as when (in imagination) he was tying the legs of a Regicide under the belly of an ass. And when in the manner of a bookseller's hack he compiled a ***Comical and Tragical History of the Lives and Adventures of the most noted Bayliffs,*** his adoration of the Royalists persuaded him to miss his chance. So brave a spirit as himself should not have looked complacently upon the officers of the law, but he saw in the glorification of the bayliff another chance of castigating the Roundheads, and thus he set an honorific crown upon the brow of man's natural enemy. "These unsanctified rascals," wrote he, "would run into any man's debt without paying him, and if their creditors were Cavaliers they thought they had as much right to cheat'em, as the Israelites had to spoil the Egyptians of their ear-rings and jewels." Alas! the boot was ever on the other leg; and yet you cannot but admire the Captain's valiant determination to sacrifice probability to his legitimate hate.

Of his declining years and death there is no record. But one likes to think of him released from care, and surrounded by books, flowers, and the good things of this earth. Now and again, maybe, he would muse on the stirring deeds of his youth, and more often he would put away the memory of action to delight in the masterpiece which made him immortal. He would recall with pleasure, no doubt, the ready praise of Richard Steele, his most appreciative reviewer, and smile contemptuously at the baseness of his friend and successor, Captain Charles Johnson. Now, this ingenious writer was wont to boast, when the ale of Fleet Steeet had empurpled his nose, that he was the most intrepid highwayman of them all. "Once upon a time," he would shout, with an arrogant gesture, "I was known from Blackheath to Hounslow, from Ware to Shooter's Hill." But the truth is, the only "crime" he ever committed was plagiarism. The self-assumed title of Captain should have deceived nobody, for the braggart never stole anything more difficult of acquisition than another man's words. He picked brains, not pockets; he committed the greater sin and ran no risk. He helped himself to the admirable inventions of Captain Smith without apology or acknowledgment, and as though to lighten the dead-weight of his sin, he never skipped an opportunity of maligning his victim. Again and again in the very act to steal he will declare vain-gloriously that Captain Smith's stories are "barefaced inventions." But doubt was no check to the habit of plunder, and you knew that at every reproach, expressed (so to say) in self-defence, he plied the scissors with the greater energy. The most cunning theft is the tag which adorns the title-page of his book:

Little villains oft submit to fate That great ones may enjoy the world in state.

Thus he quotes from Gay, and you applaud the aptness of the quotation, until you discover that already it was used by Steele in his appreciation of the heroic Smith! However, Johnson has his uses, and those to whom the masterpiece of Captain Alexander is inaccessible will turn with pleasure to the *General History of the Lives and Adventures of the most Famous Highwaymen, Murderers, Street-Robbers, Etc.,* and will feel no regret that for once they are receiving stolen goods.

Though Johnson fell immeasurably below his predecessor in talent, he manifestly excelled him in scholarship. A sojourn at the University had supplied him with a fine assortment of Latin tags, and he delighted to prove his erudition by the citation of the Chronicles. Had he possessed a sense of humour, he might have smiled at the irony of committing a theft upon the historian of thieves. But he was too vain and too pompous to smile at his own weakness, and thus he would pretend himself a venturesome highwayman, a brave writer, and a profound scholar. Indeed, so far did his pride carry him, that he would have the world believe him the same Charles Johnson, who wrote *The Gentleman Cully and The Successful Pyrate.* Thus with a boastful chuckle he would quote:

Johnson, who now to sense, now nonsense leaning, Means not, but blunders round about a meaning.

Thus, ignoring the insult, he would plume himself after his drunken fashion that he, too, was an enemy of Pope.

Yet Johnson has remained an example. For the literature of scoundrelism is as persistent in its form as in its folk-lore. As Harman's *Caveat,* which first saw the light in 1566, serves as a model to an unbroken series of such books, as *The London Spy*, so from Johnson in due course were developed the *Newgate Calendar*, and those innumerable records, which the latter half of the Eighteenth Century furnished us forth. The celebrated Calendar was in its origin nothing more than a list of prisoners printed in a folia slip. But thereafter it became the *Malefactors' Bloody Register*, which we know. Its plan and purpose were to improve the occasion. The thief is no longer esteemed for an artist or appraised upon his merits: he is the awful warning, which shall lead the sinner to repentance. "Here," says the preface, "the giddy thoughtless youth may see as in a mirror the fatal consequences of deviating from virtue"; here he may tremble at the discovery that "often the best talents are prostituted to the basest purposes." But in spite of "the proper reflections of the whole affair," the famous *Calendar* deserved the praise of Borrow. There is a directness in the narration, which captures all those for whom life and literature are something better than psychologic formulæ. Moreover, the motives which drive the brigand to his doom are brutal in their simplicity, and withal as genuine and sincere as greed, vanity, and lust can make them. The true amateur takes pleasure even in the pious exhortations, because he knows that they crawl into their place, lest the hypocrite be scandalised. But with years the *Newgate Calendar* also declined, and at last it has followed other dead literatures into the night.

Meanwhile the broadsheet had enjoyed an unbroken and prosperous career. Up and down London, up and down England, hurried the Patterer or Flying Stationer. There was no murder, no theft, no conspiracy, which did not tempt the Gutter Muse to doggerel. But it was not until James Catnach came up from Alnwick to London (in 1813), that the trade reached the top of its prosperity. The vast sheets, which he published with their scurvy couplets, and the admirable woodcut, serving in its time for a hundred executions, have not lost their power to fascinate. Theirs is the aspect of the early woodcut; the coarse-cut type and the catchpenny headlines are a perpetual delight; as you unfold them, your care keeps pace with your admiration; and you cannot feel them crackle beneath your hand without enthusiasm and without regret. He was no pedant—Jemmy Catnach; and the image of his ruffians was commonly as far from portraiture, as his verses were remote from poetry. But he put together in a roughly artistic shape the last murder, robbery, or scandal of the day. His masterpieces were far too popular to live, and if they knew so vast a circulation as 2,500,000 they are hard indeed to come by. And now the art is well-nigh dead; though you may discover an infrequent survival in a country town. But how should Catnach, were he alive to-day, compete with the Special Edition of an evening print?

The decline of the Scoundrel, in feet, has been followed by the disappearance of chap-book and broadsheet. The Education Act, which made the cheap novel a necessity, destroyed at a blow the literature of the street. Since the highwayman wandered, fur-coated, into the City, the patterer has lost his occupation. Robbery and murder have degenerated into Chinese puzzles, whose solution is a pleasant irritant to the idle brain. The misunderstanding of Poe has produced a vast polyglot literature, for which one would not give in exchange a single chapter of Captain Smith. Vautrin and Bill Sykes are already discredited, and it is a false reflection of M. Dupin, which dazzles the eye of a moral and unimaginative world. Yet the wise man sighs for those fearless days, when the brilliant Macheath rode vizarded down Shooter's Hill, and presently saw his exploits set forth, with the proper accompaniment of a renowned and ancient woodcut, upon a penny broadsheet.

CAPTAIN HIND

JAMES HIND, the Master Thief of England, the fearless Captain of the Highway, was born at Chipping Norton in 1618. His father, a simple saddler, had so poor an appreciation of his son's magnanimity, that he apprenticed him to a butcher; but Hind's destiny was to embrue his hands in other than the blood of oxen, and he had not long endured the restraint of this common craft when forty shillings, the gift of his mother, purchased him an escape, and carried him triumphant and ambitious to London.

Even in his negligent schooldays he had fastened upon a fitting career. A born adventurer, he sought only enterprise and command: if a commission in the army failed him, then he would risk his neck upon the road, levying his own tax and imposing his own conditions. To one of his dauntless resolution an opportunity need never have lacked; yet he owed his first preferment to a happy accident. Surprised one evening in a drunken brawl, he was hustled into the Poultry Counter, and there made acquaintance over a fresh bottle with Robert Allen, one of the chief rogues in the Park, and a ruffian, who had mastered every trick in the game of plunder. A dexterous cly-faker, an intrepid blade, Allen had also the keenest eye for untested talent, and he detected Hind's shining qualities after the first glass. No sooner had they paid the price of release, than Hind was admitted of his comrade's gang; he took the oath of fealty, and by way of winning his spurs was bid to hold up a travel-ler on Shooter's Hill. Granted his choice of a mount, he straightway took the finest in the stable, with that keen perception of horse-flesh which never deserted him, and he confronted his first victim in the liveliest of humours. There was no falter in his voice, no hint of inexperience in his manner, when he shouted the battle-cry: "Stand and deliver"! The horseman, fearful of his life, instantly surrendered a purse of ten sovereigns, as to the most practised assailant on the road. Whereupon Hind, with a flourish of ancient courtesy, gave him twenty shillings to bear his charges. "This," said he, "is for handsale sake" and thus they parted in mutual compliment and content.

Allen was overjoyed at his novice's prowess. "Did you not see," he cried to his companions, "how he robbed him with a grace?" And well did the trooper deserve his captain's compliment, for his art was perfect from the first. In bravery as in gal-lantry he knew no rival, and he plundered with so elegant a style, that only a churl-ish victim could resent the extortion. He would as soon have turned his back upon an enemy as demand a purse uncovered. For every man he had a quip, for every woman a compliment; nor did he ever conceal the truth that the means were for him as important as the end. Though he loved money, he still insisted that it should be yielded in freedom and good temper; and while he emptied more coaches than any man in England, he was never at a loss for admirers.

Under Allen he served a brilliant apprenticeship. Enrolled as a servant, he speedily sat at the master's right hand, and his nimble brains devised many a pretty campaign. For a while success dogged the horse-hoofs of the gang; with wealth came immunity, and not one of the warriors had the misfortune to look out upon the world through a grate. They robbed with dignity, even with splendour. Now they would drive forth in a coach and four, carrying with them a whole armoury of offensive weapons; now they would take the road apparelled as noblemen, and attended at a discreet distance by their proper servants. But recklessness brought the inevitable disaster; and it was no less a personage than Oliver Cromwell who overcame the hitherto invincible Allen. A handful of the gang attacked Oliver on his way from Huntingdon, but the marauders were outmatched, and the most of them were forced to surrender. Allen, taken red-handed, swung at Tyburn, but Hind, with his better mount and defter horsemanship, rode clear away.

The loss of his friend was a lesson in caution, and henceforth Hind resolved to follow his craft in solitude. He had embellished his native talent with all the instruction that others could impart, and he reflected that he who rode alone neither ran risk of discovery nor had any need to share his booty. Thus he begun his easy, untrammelled career, making time and space of no account by his rapid, fearless journeys. Now he was prancing the moors of Yorkshire, now he was scouring the plain between Gloucester and Tewkesbury, but wherever he rode, he had a purse in his pocket and a jest on his tongue. To recall his prowess is to ride with him (in fancy) under the open sky along the fair, beaten road; to put up with him at the white, busy posthouse, to drink unnumbered pints of mulled sack with the round-bellied landlord, to exchange boastful stories over the hospitable fire, and to ride forth in the morning with the joyous uncertainty of travel upon you. Failure alone lay outside his experience, and he presently became at once the terror and the hero of England.

Not only was his courage conspicuous; luck also was his constant companion; and a happy bewitchment protected him for three years against the possibility of harm. He had been lying at Hatfield, at the George Inn, and set out in the early morning for London. As he neared the town-gate, an old beldame begged an alms of him, and though Hind, not liking her ill-favoured visage, would have spurred forward, the beldame's glittering eye held his horse motionless. "Good woman," cried Hind, flinging her a crown, "I am in haste; pray let me pass." "Sir," answered the witch, "three days I have awaited your coming. Would you have me lose my labour now?" And with Hind's assent the sphinx delivered her message: "Captain Hind," said she, "your life is beset with constant danger, and since from your birth I have wished you well, my poor skill has devised a perfect safeguard." With this she gave him a small box containing what might have been a sundial or compass. "Watch this star," quoth she, "and when you know not your road, follow its guidance. Thus you shall be preserved from every peril for the space of three years. Thereafter, if you still have faith in my devotion, seek me again, and I will renew the virtue of the charm."

Hind took the box joyfully; but when he turned to murmur a word of gratitude, the witch struck his nag's flanks with a white wand, the horse leapt vehemently forward, and Hind saw his benefactress no more. Henceforth, however, a warning voice spoke to him as plainly as did the demon to Socrates; and had he but obeyed the beldame's admonition, he might have escaped a violent death. For he passed the last day of the third year at the siege of Youghal, where, deprived of happy guidance, he was seriously wounded, and whence he presently regained England to his own undoing.

So long as he kept to the road, his life was one long comedy. His wit and address were inexhaustible, and fortune never found him at a loss. He would avert suspicion with the tune of a psalm, as when, habited like a pious shepherd, he broke a traveller's head with his crook, and deprived him of his horse. An early adventure was to force a pot-valiant parson, who had drunk a cup too much at a wedding, into a rarely farcical situation. Hind, having robbed two gentlemen's servants of a round sum, went ambling along the road until he encountered a parson. "Sir," said he, "I am closely pursued by robbers. You, I dare swear, will not stand by and see me plundered." Before the parson could protest, he thrust a pistol into his hand, and bade him fire it at the first comer, while he rode off to raise the county. Meanwhile the rifled travellers came up with the parson, who, straightway, mistaking them for thieves, fired without effect, and then, riding forward, flung the pistol in the face of the nearest. Thus the parson of the parish was dragged before the magistrate, while Hind, before his dupe could furnish an explanation, had placed many a mile between himself and his adversary.

But though he could on occasion show a clean pair of heels, Hind was never lacking in valiance; and, another day, meeting a traveller with a hundred pounds in his pocket, he challenged him to fight there and then, staked his own horse against the money, and declared that he should win who drew first blood. "If I am the conqueror," said the magnanimous Captain, "I will give you ten pounds for your journey. If you are favoured of fortune, you shall give me your servant's horse." The terms were instantly accepted, and in two minutes Hind had run his adversary through the sword-arm. But finding that his victim was but a poor squire going to

London to pay his composition, he not only returned his money, but sought him out a surgeon, and gave him the best dinner the countryside could afford.

Thus it was his pleasure to act as a providence, many a time robbing Peter to pay Paul, and stripping the niggard that he might indulge his fervent love of generosity. Of all usurers and bailiffs he had a wholesome horror, and merry was the prank which he played upon the extortionate moneylender of Warwick. Riding on an easy rein through the town, Hind heard a tumult at a street corner, and inquiring the cause, was told that an innkeeper was arrested by a thievish usurer for a paltry twenty pounds. Dismounting, this providence in jack-boots discharged the debt, cancelled the bond, and took the innkeeper's goods for his own security. And thereupon overtaking the usurer, "My friend!" he exclaimed, "I lent you late a sum of twenty pounds. Repay it at once, or I take your miserable life." The usurer was obliged to return the money, with another twenty for interest, and when he would take the law of the innkeeper, was shown the bond duly cancelled, and was flogged well-nigh to death for his pains.

So Hind rode the world up and down, redressing grievances like an Eastern monarch, and rejoicing in the abasement of the evildoer. Nor was the spirit of his adventure bounded by the ocean. More than once he crossed the seas; the Hague knew him, and Amsterdam, though these somnolent cities gave small occasion for the display of his talents. It was from Scilly that he crossed to the Isle of Man, where, being recommended to Lord Derby, he gained high favour, and received in exchange for his jests a comfortable stipend. Hitherto, said the Chronicles, thieving was unknown in the island. A man might walk whither he would, a bag of gold in one hand, a switch in the other, and fear no danger. But no sooner had Hind appeared at Douglas than honest citizens were pilfered at every turn. In dismay they sought the protection of the Governor, who instantly suspected Hind, and gallantly disclosed his suspicions to the Captain. "My lord!" exclaimed Hind, a blush upon his cheek, a I protest my innocence; but willingly will I suffer the heaviest penalty of your law if I am recognised for the thief." The victims, confronted with their robber, knew him not, picturing to the Governor a monster with long hair and unkempt beard. Hind, acquitted with apologies, fetched from his lodging the disguise of periwig and beard. "They laugh who win!" he murmured, and thus forced forgiveness and a chuckle even from his judges.

As became a gentleman-adventurer, Captain Hind was staunch in his loyalty to his murdered King. To strip the wealthy was always reputable, but to rob a Regicide was a masterpiece of well-doing. A fervent zeal to lighten Cromwell's pocket had brought the illustrious Allen to the gallows. But Hind was not one whit abashed, and he would never forego the chance of an encounter with his country's enemies. His treatment of Hugh Peters in Enfield Chace is among his triumphs. At the first encounter the Presbyterian plucked up courage enough to oppose his adversary with texts. To Hind's command of a Stand and deliver!" duly enforced with a loaded pistol, the ineffable Peters replied with ox-eye sanctimoniously upturned: "Thou shalt not steal; let him that stole, steal no more," adding thereto other variations of the eighth commandment. Hind immediately countered with exhortations against the awful sin of murder, and rebuked the blasphemy of the Regicides, who, to defend their own infamy, would wrest Scripture from its meaning. "Did you not, O monster of impiety," mimicked Hind in the preacher's own voice, "pervert for your own advantage the words of the Psalmist, who said, 'Bind their kings with chains, and their nobles with fetters of iron'? Moreover, was it not Solomon who wrote: 'Men do not despise a thief, if he steal to satisfy his soul when he is hungry'? And is not my soul hungry for gold and the Regicides' discomfiture?" Peters was still fumbling after texts when the final argument: a Deliver thy money, or I will send thee out of the world!" frightened him into submission, and thirty broad pieces were Hind's reward.

Not long afterwards he confronted Bradshaw near Sherborne, and having taken from him a purse fat with Jacobuses he bade the Sergeant stand uncovered, while he delivered a discourse upon gold, thus shaped by tradition: "Ay, marry, sir, this is the metal that wins my heart for ever! O precious gold, I admire and adore thee as much as Bradshaw, Prynne, or any villain of the same stamp. This is that incomparable medicament, which the republican physicians call the wonderworking plaster. It is truly catholic in operation, and somewhat akin to the Jesuit's powder, but more effectual. The virtues of it are strange and various; it makes justice deaf as well as blind, and takes out spots of the deepest treason more cleverly than castle-soap does common stains; it alters a man's constitution in two or three days, more than the virtuoso's transfusion of blood can do in seven years. 'Tis a great alexio-pharmick, and helps poisonous principles of rebellion, and those that use them. It miraculously exalts and purifies the eyesight, and makes traitors behold nothing but innocence in the blackest malefactors. 'Tis a mighty cordial for a declining cause; it stifles faction or schism, as certainly as the itch is destroyed by butter and brimstone. In a word, it makes wise men fools, and fools wise men, and both knaves. The very colour of this precious balm is bright and dazzling. If it be properly applied to the fist, that is in a decent manner, and a competent dose, it infallibly performs all the cures which the evils of humanity crave." Thus having spoken, he killed the six horses of Bradshaw's coach, and went contemptuously on his way.

But he was not a Cavalier merely in sympathy, nor was he content to prove his loyalty by robbing Roundheads. He, too, would strike a blow for his King, and he showed, first with the royal army in Scotland, and afterwards at Worcester, what he dared in a righteous cause. Indeed, it was his part in the unhappy battle that cost him his life, and there is a strange irony in the reflection that, on the self-same day whereon Sir Thomas Urquhart lost his precious manuscripts in Worcester's kennels, the neck of James Hind was made ripe for the halter. His capture was due to treachery. Towards the end of 1651 he was lodged with one Denzys, a barber, over against St. Dunstan's Church in Fleet Street. Maybe he had chosen his hiding-place for its neighbourhood to Moll Cutpurse's own sanctuary. But a pack of traitors discovered him, and haling him before the Speaker of the House of Commons, got him committed forthwith to Newgate.

At first he was charged with theft and murder, and was actually condemned for killing George Sympson at Knole in Berkshire. But the day after his sentence, an Act of Oblivion was passed, and Hind was put upon trial for treason. During his examination he behaved with the utmost gaiety, boastfully enlarging upon his services to the King's cause. "These are filthy jingling spurs," said he as he left the bar, pointing to the irons about his legs, "but I hope to exchange them ere long." His good-humour remained with him to the end. He jested in prison as he jested on the road, and it was with a light heart that he mounted the scaffold built for him at Worcester. His was the fate reserved for traitors: he was hanged, drawn, and quartered, and though his head was privily stolen and buried on the day of execution, his quarters were displayed upon the town walls, until time and the birds destroyed them utterly.

Thus died the most distinguished highwayman that ever drew rein upon an

English road; and he died the death of a hero. The unnumbered crimes of violence and robbery wherewith he might have been charged weighed not a feather's weight upon his destiny; he suffered not in the cause of plunder, but in the cause of Charles Stuart. And in thus excusing his death, his contemporaries did him scant justice. For while in treasonable loyalty he had a thousand rivals, on the road he was the first exponent of the grand manner. The middle of the seventeenth century was, in truth, the golden age of the Road. Not only were all the highwaymen Cavaliers, but many a Cavalier turned highwayman. Broken at their King's defeat, a hundred captains took pistol and vizard, and revenged themselves as freebooters upon the King's enemies. And though Hind was outlaw first and royalist afterwards, he was still the most brilliant collector of them all. True, he owed something to his master, Allen; but he added from the storehouse of his own genius a host of new precepts, and he was the first to establish an enduring tradition.

Before all things he insisted upon courtesy; a guinea stolen by an awkward ruffian was a sorry theft; levied by a gentleman of the highway it was a tribute paid to courage by generosity. Nothing would atone for an insult offered to a lady; and when it was Hind's duty to seize part of a gentlewoman's dowry on the Petersfield road, he not only pleaded his necessity in eloquent excuse, but he made many promises on behalf of knight-errantry and damsels in distress. Never would he extort a trinket to which association had given a sentimental worth; during a long career he never left any man, save a Roundhead, penniless upon the road; nor was it his custom to strip the master without giving the man a trifle for his pains. His courage, moreover, was equal to his understanding. Since he was afraid of nothing, it was not his habit to bluster when he was not determined to have his way. Once his pistol levelled, once the solemn order given, the victim must either fight or surrender; and Hind was never the man to decline a combat with any weapons and under any circumstances.

Like the true artist that he was, he neglected no detail of his craft. As he was a perfect shot, so also he was a finished horseman; and his skill not only secured him against capture, but also helped him to the theft of such horses as his necessities required, or to the exchange of a worn-out jade for a mettled prancer. Once upon a time a credulous farmer offered twenty pounds and his own gelding for the Captain's mount. Hind struck a bargain at once, and as they jogged along the road he persuaded the farmer to set his newly-purchased horse at the tallest hedge, the broadest ditch. The bumpkin failed, as Hind knew he would fail; and, begging the loan for an instant of his ancient steed, Hind not only showed what horsemanship could accomplish, but straightway rode off with the better horse and twenty pounds in, his pocket. So marvellously did his reputation grow, that it became a distinction to be outwitted by him, and the brains of innocent men were racked to invent tricks which might have been put upon them by the illustrious Captain. Thus livelier jests and madder exploits were fathered upon him than upon any of his kind, and he has remained for two centuries the prime favourite of the chap-books.

Robbing alone, he could afford to despise pedantry: did he meet a traveller who amused his fancy he would give him the pass-word ("the fiddler's paid," or what not), as though the highway had not its code of morals; nor did he scruple, when it served his purpose, to rob the bunglers of his own profession. By this means, indeed, he raised the standard of the Road and warned the incompetent to embrace an easier trade. While he never took a shilling without sweetening his depredation with a joke, he was, like all humourists, an acute philosopher. "Remember what I tell you," he said to the foolish persons who once attempted to rob him, the master-thief of England, "disgrace not yourself for small sums, but aim high, and for great ones; the least will bring you to the gallows." There, in five lines, is the whole philosophy of thieving, and many a poor devil has leapt from the cart to his last dance because he neglected the counsel of the illustrious Hind. Among his aversions were lawyers and thief-catchers. "Truly I could wish," he exclaimed in court, "that full-fed fees were as little used in England among lawyers as the eating of swine's flesh was among the Jews." When you remember the terms of friendship whereon he lived with Moll Cutpurse, his hatred of the thief-catcher, who would hang his brother for "the lucre of ten pounds, which is the reward," or who would swallow a false oath "as easily as one would swallow buttered fish," is a trifle mysterious. But perhaps before his death an estrangement divided Hind and Moll. Was it that the Roaring Girl was too anxious to take the credit of Hind's success? Or did he harbour the unjust suspicion that when the last descent was made upon him at the barber's, Moll might have given a friendly warning?

Of this he made no confession, but the honest thief was ever a liberal hater of spies and attorneys, and Hind's prudence is unquestioned. A miracle of intelligence, a master of style, he excelled all his contemporaries and set up for posterity an unattainable standard. The eighteenth century flattered him by its imitation; but cowardice and swagger compelled it to limp many a dishonourable league behind. Despite the single inspiration of dancing a corant upon the green, Claude Duval, compared to Hind, was an empty braggart. Captain Stafford spoiled the best of his effects with a more than brutal vice. Neither Mull-Sack nor the Golden Farmer, for all their long life and handsome plunder, are comparable for an instant to the robber of Peters and Bradshaw. They kept their fist fiercely upon the gold of others, and cared not by what artifice it was extorted. But Hind never took a sovereign meanly; he approached no enterprise which he did not adorn. Living in a true Augustan age, he was a classic among highwaymen, the very Virgil of the Pad.

MOLL CUTPURSE AND JONATHAN WILD

I
MOLL CUTPURSE

THE most illustrious woman of an illustrious age, Moll Cutpurse, has never lacked the recognition due to her genius. She was scarce of age when the town devoured in greedy admiration the first record of her pranks and exploits. A year later Middleton made her the heroine of a sparkling comedy. Thereafter she became the favourite of the rufflers, the common-place of the poets. Newgate knew her, and Fleet Street; her manly figure was as familiar in the Bear Garden as at the Devil Tavern; courted alike by the thief and his victim, for fifty years she lived a life brilliant as sunlight, many-coloured as a rainbow. And she is remembered, after the lapse of centuries, not only as the Queen Regent of Misrule, the benevolent tyrant of cly-filers and heavers, of hacks and blades, but as the incomparable Roaring Girl, free of the playhouse, who perchance presided with Ben Jonson over the Parliament of Wits.

She was born in the Barbican at the heyday of England's greatness, four years after the glorious defeat of the Armada, and had to her father an honest shoemaker. She came into the world (saith rumour) with her fist doubled, and even in the cradle gave proof of a boyish, boisterous disposition. Her girlhood, if the word be not an affront to her mannish character, was as tempestuous as a wind-blown petticoat. A very "tomrig and rump-scuttle," she knew only the sports of boys: her warlike spirit counted no excuse too slight for a battle; and so valiant a lad was she of her hands, so well skilled in cudgel-play, that none ever wrested a victory from fighting Moll. While other girls were content to hem a kerchief or mark a sampler, Moll would escape to the Bear Garden, and there enjoy the sport of baiting, whose loyal patron she remained unto the end. That which most bitterly affronted her was the magpie talk of the wenches. "Why," she would ask in a fury of indignation, "why crouch over the fire with a pack of gossips, when the highway invites you to romance? Why finger a distaff, when a quarterstaff comes more aptly to your hand?"

And thus she grew in age and stature, a stranger to the soft delights of her sex, her heart still deaf to the trivial voice of love. Had not a wayward accident cumbered her with a kirtle, she would: have sought death or glory in the wars; she would have gone with Colonel Downe's men upon the road; she would have sailed to the Spanish Main for pieces of eight. But the tyranny of womanhood was as yet supreme, and the honest shoemaker, ignorant of his daughter's talent, bade her take service at a respectable saddler's, and thus suppress the frowardness of her passion. Her rebellion was instant. Never would she abandon the sword and the wrestling-booth for the harmless bodkin and the hearthstone of domesticity. Being absolute in refusal, she was kidnapped by her friends and sent on board a ship, bound for Virginia and slavery. There, in the dearth of womankind, even so sturdy a wench as Moll might have found a husband; but the enterprise was little to her taste, and, always resourceful, she escaped from shipboard before the captain had weighed his anchor. Henceforth she resolved her life should be free and chainless as the winds. Never more should needle and thread tempt her to a womanish inactivity. As Hercules, whose counterpart she was, changed his club for the distaff of Omphale, so would she put off the wimple and bodice of her sex for jerkin and galligaskins. If she could not allure manhood, then would she brave it. And though she might not cross swords with her country's foes, at least she might levy tribute upon the unjustly rich, and confront an enemy wherever there was a full pocket. Her entrance into a gang of thieves was beset by no difficulty. The Bear Garden, always her favourite resort, had made her acquainted with all the divers and rumpads of the town. The time, moreover, was favourable to enterprise, and once again was genius born into a golden age. The cutting of purses was an art brought to perfection, and already the more elegant practice of picking pockets was understood. The transition gave scope for endless ingenuity, and Moll was not slow in mastering the theory of either craft. It was a changing fashion of dress which forced a new tactic upon the thief; the pocket was invented, maybe, because the hanging purse was too easy a prey for the thievish scissors. But no sooner did the world conceal its wealth in pockets than the cly-filer was born to extract the booty with his long, nimble fingers. The trick was managed with an admirable forethought, which has been a constant example to after ages. The file was always accompanied by a bulk, whose duty it was to jostle and distract the victim while his pockets were rifled. The bung, or what not, was rapidly passed on to the attendant rub, who scurried off before the cry of ***Stop thief!*** could be raised.

Thus was the craft of thieving practised when Moll was enrolled a humble member of the gang. Yet nature had not endowed her with the qualities which ensure an active triumph. "The best signs and marks of a happy, industrious hand," wrote the hoyden, "is a long middle finger, equally suited with that they call the fool's or first finger." Now, though she was never a clumsy jade, the practice of sword-play and quarterstaff had not refined the industry of her hands, which were the rather framed for strength than for delicacy. So that though she served a willing apprenticeship, and eagerly shared the risks of her chosen trade, the fear of Newgate and Tyburn weighed heavily upon her spirit, and she cast about her for a method of escape. But avoiding the danger of discovery, she was loth to forego her just profit, and hoped that intelligence might atone for her sturdy, inactive fingers. Already she had endeared herself to the gang by unnumbered acts of kindness and generosity; already her inflexible justice had made her umpire in many a difficult dispute. If a rascal could be bought off at the gallows' foot, there was Moll with an open purse; and so speedily did she penetrate all the secrets of thievish policy, that her counsel and comfort were soon indispensable.

Here, then, was her opportunity. Always a diplomatist rather than a general, she gave up the battlefield for the council chamber. She planned the robberies which defter hands achieved; and, turning herself from cly-filer to fence, she received and changed to money all the watches and trinkets stolen by the gang. Were a citizen robbed upon the highway, he straightway betook himself to Moll, and his property was presently returned him at a handsome price. Her house, in short, became a brokery. Hither the blades and divers brought their purchases, and sought the ransom; hither came the outraged victims to buy again the jewels and rings which thievish fingers had pinched. With prosperity her method improved, until at last her statesmanship controlled the remotest details of the craft. Did one of her gang get to work overnight and carry off a wealthy swag, she had due intelligence of the affair betimes next morning, so that, furnished with an inventory of the booty, she might make a just division, or be prepared for the advent of the rightful owner.

So she gained a complete ascendency over her fellows. And once her position was assured, she came forth a pitiless autocrat. Henceforth the gang existed for her pleasure, not she for the gang's; and she was as urgent to punish insubordination as is an empress to avenge the heinous sin of treason. The pickpocket who had claimed her protection knew no more the delight of freedom. If he dared conceal the booty that was his, he had an enemy more powerful than the law, and many a time did contumacy pay the last penalty at the gallows. But the faithful also had their reward, for Moll never deserted a comrade, and while she lived in perfect safety herself she knew well how to contrive the safety of others. Nor was she content merely to discharge those duties of the fence for which an instinct of statecraft designed her. Her restless brain seethed with plans of plunder, and if her hands were idle it was her direction that emptied half the pockets in London. Having drilled her army of divers to an unparalleled activity, she cast about for some fresh method of warfare, and so enrolled a regiment of heavers, who would lurk at the mercers' doors for an opportunity to carry off ledgers and account-books. The price of redemption was fixed by Moll herself, and until the mercers were aroused by frequent losses to a quicker vigilance, the trade was profitably secure.

Meanwhile new clients were ever seeking her aid, and, already empress of the thieves, she presently aspired to the friendship and patronage of the highwaymen. Though she did not dispose of their booty, she was appointed their banker, and vast was the treasure entrusted to the coffers of honest Moll. Now, it was her pride to keep only the best company, for she hated stupidity worse than a clumsy hand, and they were men of wit and spirit who frequented her house. Thither came the famous Captain Hind, the Regicides' inveterate enemy, whose lofty achievements Moll, with an amiable extravagance, was wont to claim for her own. Thither came the unamiably notorious Mull Sack, who once emptied Cromwell's pocket on the Mall, and whose courage was as formidable as his rough-edged tongue. Another favourite was the ingenious Crowder, whose humour it was to take the road habited like a bishop, and who surprised the victims of his greed with ghostly counsel. Thus it was a merry party that assembled in the lady's parlour, loyal to the memory of the martyred king, and quick to fling back an offending pleasantry.

But the house in Fleet Street was a refuge as well as a resort, the sanctuary of a hundred rascals, whose misdeeds were not too flagrantly discovered. For, while Moll always allowed discretion to govern her conduct, while she would risk no present security for a vague promise of advantages to come, her secret influence in Newgate made her more powerful than the hangman and the whole bench of judges. There was no turnkey who was not her devoted servitor, but it was the clerk of Newgate to whom she and her family where most deeply beholden. This was one Ralph Briscoe, as pretty a fellow as ever deserted the law for a bull-baiting. Though wizened and clerkly in appearance, he was of a high stomach; and Moll was heard to declare that had she not been sworn to celibacy, she would have cast an eye upon the faithful Ralph, who was obedient to her behests whether at Gaol Delivery or Bear Garden. For her he would pack a jury or get a reprieve; for him she would bait a bull with the fiercest dogs in London. Why then should she fear the law, when the clerk of Newgate and Gregory the Hangman fought upon her side?

For others the arbiter of life and death, she was only thrice in an unexampled career confronted with the law. Her first occasion of arrest was so paltry that it brought discredit only on the constable. This jack-in-office, a very Dogberry, encountered Moll returning down Ludgate Hill from some merry-making, a lanthorn carried pompously before her. Startled by her attire he questioned her closely, and receiving insult for answer, promptly carried her to the Round House. The customary garnish made her free of the prison, and next morning a brief interview with the Lord Mayor restored Moll to liberty but not to forgetfulness. She had yet to wreak her vengeance upon the constable for a monstrous affront, and hearing presently that he had a rich uncle in Shropshire, she killed the old gentleman (in imagination) and made the constable his heir. Instantly a retainer, in the true garb and accent of the country, carried the news to Dogberry, and sent him off to Ludlow on the costliest of fool's errands. He purchased a horse and set forth joyously, as became a man of property, but he limped home, broken in purse and spirit, the hapless object of ridicule and contempt. Perhaps he guessed the author of this sprightly outrage; but Moll, for her part, was far too finished a humourist to reveal the truth, and hereafter she was content to swell the jesting chorus.

Her second encounter with justice was no mere pleasantry, and it was only her marvellous generalship that snatched her career from untimely ruin and herself from the clutch of Master Gregory. Two of her emissaries had encountered a farmer in Chancery Lane. They spoke with him first at Smithfield, and knew that his pocket was well lined with bank-notes. An improvised quarrel at a tavern-door threw the farmer off his guard, and though he defended the money, his watch was snatched from his fob and duly carried to Moll. The next day the victim, anxious to repurchase his watch, repaired to Fleet Street, where Moll generously promised to recover the stolen property. But unhappily security had encouraged recklessness, and as the farmer turned to leave he espied his own watch hanging among other trinkets upon the wall. With a rare discretion he held his peace until he had called a constable to his aid, and this time the Roaring Girl was lodged in Newgate, with an ugly crime laid to her charge.

Committed for trial, she demanded that the watch should be left in the constable's keeping, and, pleading not guilty when the sessions came round, insisted that her watch and the farmer's were not the same. The farmer, anxious to acknowledge his property, demanded the constable to deliver the watch, that it might be sworn to in open court; but when the constable put his hand to his pocket the only piece of damning evidence had vanished, stolen by the nimble fingers of one of Moll's officers. Thus with admirable trickery and a perfect sense of dramatic effect she contrived her escape, and never again ran the risk of a sudden discovery. For experience brought caution in its train, and though this wiliest of fences lived almost within the shadow of Newgate, though she was as familiar in the prison yard as at the Globe Tavern, her nightly resort, she obeyed the rules of life and law with so precise an exactitude that suspicion could never fasten upon her. Her kingdom was midway between robbery and justice. And as she controlled the mystery of thieving so, in reality, she meted out punishment to the evildoer. Honest citizens were robbed with small risk to life or property. For Moll always frowned upon violence, and was ever ready to restore the booty for a fair ransom. And the thieves, driven by discipline to a certain humanity, plied their trade with an obedience and orderliness hitherto unknown. Moll's then was no mean achievement. But her career was not circumscribed by her trade, and the Roaring Girl, the dare-devil companion of the wits and bloods, enjoyed a fame no less glorious than the Queen of Thieves.

"Enter Moll in a frieze jerkin and a black safeguard." Thus in the old comedy she comes upon the stage; and truly it was by her clothes that she was first notorious. By accident a woman, by habit a man, she must needs invent a costume proper to her pursuits. But she was no shrieking reformer, no fanatic spying regeneration in a pair of breeches. Only in her attire she showed her wit; and she went to a bull-baiting in such a dress as well became her favourite sport. She was not of those who "walk in spurs but never ride." The jerkin, the doublet, the galligaskins were put on to serve the practical purposes of life, not to attract the policeman or the spinster. And when a petticoat spread its ample folds beneath the doublet, not only was her array handsome, but it symbolised the career of one who was neither man nor woman, and yet both. After a while, however, the petticoat seemed too tame for her stalwart temper, and she exchanged it for the great Dutch slop, habited in which unseemly garment she is pictured in the ancient prints.

Up and down the town she romped and scolded, earning the name which Middleton gave her in her green girlhood. "She has the spirit of four great parishes," says the wit in the comedy, "and a voice that will drown all the city." If a gallant stood in the way she drew upon him in an instant, and he must be a clever swordsman to hold his ground against the tomboy who had laid low the German fencer himself. A good fellow always, she had ever a merry word for the passer-by, and so sharp was her tongue that none ever put a trick upon her, Not to know Moll was to be inglorious, and she "slipped from one company to another like a fat eel between a Dutchman's fingers." Now at Parker's Ordinary, now at the Bear Garden, she frequented only the haunts of men, and not until old age came upon her did she endure patiently the presence of women.

Her voice and speech were suited to the galligaskin. She was a true disciple of Maître Francois, hating nothing so much as mincing obscenity, and if she flavoured her discourse with many a blasphemous quip, the blasphemy was "not so malicious as customary." Like the blood she was, she loved good ale and wine; and she regarded it among her proudest titles to renown that she was the first of women to smoke tobacco. Many was the pound of best Virginian that she bought of Mistress Gallipot, and the pipe, with monkey, dog, and eagle, is her constant emblem. Her antic attire, the fearless courage of her pranks, now and again involved her in disgrace or even jeopardised her freedom; but her unchanging gaiety made light of disaster, and still she laughed and rollicked in defiance of prude and pedant.

Her companion in many a fantastical adventure was Banks, the vintner of Cheapside, that same Banks who taught his horse to dance and shod him with silver. Now once upon a time a right witty sport was devised between them. The vintner bet Moll £20 that she would not ride from Charing Cross to Shore-ditch astraddle on horseback, in breeches and doublet, boots, and spurs. The hoyden took him up in a moment, and added of her own devilry a trumpet and banner. She set out from Charing Cross bravely enough, and a trumpeter being an unwonted spectacle, the eyes of all the town were clapped upon her. Yet none knew her until she reached Bishopsgate, where an orange-wench set up the cry, "Moll Cutpurse on horseback"! Instantly the cavalier was surrounded by a noisy mob. Some would have torn her from the saddle for an imagined insult upon womanhood, others, more wisely minded, laughed at the prank with good-humoured merriment. But every minute the throng grew denser, and it had fared hardly with roystering Moll, had not a wedding and the arrest of a debtor presently distracted the gaping idlers. As the mob turned to gaze at the fresh wonder, she spurred her horse until she gained Newington by an unfrequented lane. There she waited until night should cover her progress to Shoreditch, and thus peacefully she returned home to lighten the vintner's pocket of twenty pounds.

But the fame of the adventure spread abroad, and that, the scandal should not be repeated Moll was summoned before the Court of Arches to answer a charge of appearing publicly in mannish apparel. The august tribunal had no terror for her, and she received her sentence to do penance in a white sheet at Paul's Cross during morning-service on a Sunday with an audacious contempt. "They might as well have shamed a black dog as me," she proudly exclaimed; and why should she dread the white sheet, when all the spectators looked with a lenient eye upon her professed discomfiture? " For a halfpenny," she said, "she would have travelled to every market-town of England in the guise of a penitent," and having tippled off three quarts of sack she swaggered to Paul's Cross in the maddest of humours. But not all the courts on earth could lengthen her petticoat, or contract the Dutch slop by a single fold. For a while, perhaps, she chastened her costume, yet she soon reverted to the ancient mode, and to her dying day went habited as a man.

As bear-baiting was the passion of her life, so she was scrupulous in the care and training of her dogs. She gave them each a trundle-bed, wrapping them from the cold in sheets and blankets, while their food would not have dishonoured a gentleman's table. Parrots, too, gave a sense of colour and companionship to her house; and it was in this love of pets, and her devotion to cleanliness, that she showed a trace of dormant womanhood. Abroad a ribald and a scold, at home she was the neatest of housewives, and her parlour, with its mirrors and its manifold ornaments, was the envy of the neighbours. So her trade flourished, and she lived a life of comfort, of plenty even, until the Civil War threw her out of work. When an unnatural conflict set the whole country at loggerheads, what occasion was there for the honest prig? And it is not surprising that, like all the gentlemen adventurers of the age, Moll remained most stubbornly loyal to the King's cause. She made the conduit in Fleet Street run with wine when Charles came to London in 1638; and it was her amiable pleasantry to give the name of Strafford to a clever, cunning bull, and to dub the dogs that assailed him Pym, Hampden, and the rest, that right heartily she might applaud the courage of Strafford as he threw off his unwary assailants.

So long as the quarrel lasted, she was compelled to follow a profession more ancient than the fence's; for there is one passion which war itself cannot extinguish. But once the King had laid his head "down as upon a bed," once the Protector had proclaimed his supremacy, the industry of the road revived; and there was not a single diver or rumpad that did not declare eternal war upon the black-hearted Regicides. With a laudable devotion to her chosen cause, Moll despatched the most experienced of her gang to rob Lady Fairfax on her way to church; and there is a tradition that the Roaring Girl, hearing that Fairfax would pass by Hounslow, rode forth to meet him, and with her own voice bade him stand and deliver. One would like to believe it; yet it is scarce credible. If Fairfax had spent the balance of an ignominious career in being plundered by a band of loyal brigands, he would not have had time to justify the innumerable legends of pockets emptied and pistols levelled at his head. Moreover, Moll herself was laden with years, and she had always preferred the council chamber to the battlefield. But it is certain that, with Captain Hind and Mull Sack to aid, she schemed many a clever plot against the Roundheads, and nobly she played her part in avenging the martyred King.

Thus she declined into old age, attended, like Queen Mary, by her maids, who would card, reel, spin, and beguile her leisure with sweet singing. Though her spirit was untamed, the burden of her years compelled her to a tranquil life. She, who formerly never missed a bull-baiting, must now content herself with tick-tack. Her fortune, moreover, had been wrecked in the Civil War. Though silver shells still jingled in her pocket, time was she knew the rattle of the yellow boys. But she never lost courage, and died at last of a dropsy, in placid contentment with her lot. Assuredly she was born at a time well suited to her genius. Had she lived to-day, she might have been a "Pioneer"; she might even have discussed some paltry problem of sex in a printed obscenity. In her own freer, wiser age, she was not man's detractor, but his rival; and if she never knew the passion of love, she was always loyal to the obligation of friendship. By her will she left twenty pounds to celebrate the Second Charles's restoration to his kingdom; and you contemplate her career with the single regret that she died a brief year before the red wine, thus generously bestowed, bubbled at the fountain.

II
JONATHAN WILD

WHEN Jonathan Wild and the Count La Ruse, W in Fielding's narrative, took a hand at cards, Jonathan picked his opponent's pocket, though he knew it was empty, while the Count, from sheer force of habit, stocked the cards, though Wild had not a farthing to lose. And if in his uncultured youth the great man stooped to prig with his own hand, he was early cured of the weakness: so that Fielding's picture of the hero taking a bottle-screw from the Ordinary's pocket in the very moment of death is entirely fanciful. For "this Machiavel of Thieves," as a contemporary styled him, left others to accomplish what his ingenuity had planned. His was the high policy of theft. If he lived on terms of familiar intimacy with the mill-kens, the bridle-culls, the buttock-and-files of London, he was none the less the friend and minister of justice. He enjoyed the freedom of Newgate and the Old Bailey. He came and went as he liked: he packed juries, he procured bail, he manufactured evidence; and there was scarce an assize or a sessions passed but he slew his man.

The world knew him for a robber, yet could not refuse his brilliant service. At the Poultry Counter, you are told, he laid the foundations of his future greatness, and to the Poultry Counter he was committed for some trifling debt ere he had fully served his apprenticeship to the art and mystery of buckle-making. There he learned his craft, and at his enlargement he was able forthwith to commence thief-catcher. His plan was conceived with an effrontery that was nothing less than genius. On the one side he was the factor, or rather the tyrant, of the cross-coves; on the other he was the trusted agent of justice, the benefactor of the outraged and the plundered. Among his earliest exploits was the recovery of the Countess of G—d—n's chair, impudently carried off when her ladyship had but just alighted; and the courage wherewith he brought to justice the murderers of one Mrs. Knap, who had been slain for some trifling booty, established his reputation as upon a rock. He at once advertised himself in the public prints as Thief-Catcher General of Great Britain and Ireland, and proceeded to send to the gallows every scoundrel that dared dispute his position.

His opportunities of gain were infinite. Even if he did not organise the robbery which his cunning was presently to discover, he had spies in every hole and corner to set him on the felon's track. Nor did he leave a single enterprise to chance: "He divided the city and suburbs into wards or divisions, and appointed the persons who were to attend each ward, and kept them strictly to their duty." If a subordinate dared to disobey or to shrink from murder, Jonathan hanged him at the next assize, and happily for him he had not a single confederate whose neck he might not put in the halter when he chose. Thus he preserved the union and the fidelity of his gang, punishing by judicial murder the smallest insubordination, the faintest suspicion of rivalry. Even when he had shut his victim up in Newgate, he did not leave him so long as there was a chance of blackmail. He would make the most generous offers of evidence and defence to every thief that had a stiver left him. But whether or no he kept his bargain—that depended upon policy and inclination. On one occasion, when he had brought a friend to the Old Bailey, and relented at the last moment, he kept the prosecutor drunk from the noble motive of self-interest, until the case was over. And so esteemed was he of the officers of the law that even this interference did but procure a reprimand.

His meanest action marked him out from his fellows, but it was not until he habitually pillaged the treasures he afterwards restored to their grateful owners for a handsome consideration, that his art reached the highest point of excellence.

The event was managed by him with amazing adroitness from beginning to end. It was he who discovered the wealth and habit of the victim; it was he who posted the thief and seized the plunder, giving a paltry commission to his hirelings for the trouble; it was he who kept whatever valuables were lost in the transaction; and as he was the servant of the Court, discovery or inconvenience was impossible. Surely the Machiavel of Thieves is justified of his title. He was known to all the rich and titled folk in town; and if he was generally able to give them back their stolen valuables at something more than double their value, he treated his clients with a most proper insolence. When Lady M—n was unlucky enough to lose a silver buckle at Windsor, she asked Wild to recover it, and offered the hero twenty pounds for his trouble. "Zounds, Madam," says he, "you offer nothing. It cost the gentleman who took it forty pounds for his coach, equipage, and other expenses to Windsor." His impudence increased with success, and in the geniality of his cups he was wont to boast his amazing rogueries: "hinting not without vanity at the poor Understandings of the Greatest Part of Mankind, and his own Superior Cunning."

In fifteen years he claimed £10,000 for his dividend of recovered plunderings, and who shall estimate the moneys which flowed to his treasury from blackmail and the robberies of his gang? So brisk became his trade in jewels and the precious metals that he opened relations with Holland, and was master of a fleet. His splendour increased with wealth: he carried a silver-mounted sword, and a footman tramped at his heels. "His table was very splendid," says a biographer: "he seldom dining under five Dishes, the Reversions whereof were generally charitably bestow'd on the Commonside felons." At his second marriage with Mrs. Mary D—n, the hempen widow of Scull D—n, his humour was most happily expressed: he distributed white ribbons among the turnkeys, he gave the Ordinary gloves and favours, he sent the prisoners of Newgate several ankers of brandy for punch. 'Twas a fitting complaisance, since his fortune was drawn from Newgate, and since he was destined himself, a few years later, to drink punch—"a liquor nowhere spoken against in the Scriptures"—with the same Ordinary whom he thus magnificently decorated. Endowed with considerable courage, for a while he had the prudence to save his skin, and despite his bravado he was known on occasion to yield a plundered treasure to an accomplice who set a pistol to his head. But it is certain that the accomplice died at Tyburn for his pains, and on equal terms Jonathan was resolute with the best. On the trail he was savage as a wild beast. When he arrested James Wright for a robbery committed upon the persons of the Earl of B—1—n and the Lord Bruce, he held on to the victim's chin by his teeth—an exploit which reminds you of the illustrious Tiger Roche !

Even in his lifetime he was generously styled the Great. The scourge of London, he betrayed and destroyed every man that ever dared to live upon terms of friendship with him. It was Jonathan that made Blueskin a thief,and Jonathan only screened his creature from justice so long as clemency seemed profitable. At the first hint of disobedience Blueskin was committed to Newgate. When he had stood his trial, and was being taken to the Condemned Hole, he beckoned to Wild as though to a conference, and cut his throat with a penknife. The assembled rogues and turnkeys thought their Jonathan dead at last, and rejoiced exceedingly therein. Straightway the poet of Newgate's Garland leaped into verse:

Then hopeless of life, He drew his penknife, And made a sad widow of Jonathan's wife. But forty pounds paid her, her grief shall appease, And every man round me may rob, if he please.

But Jonathan recovered, and Molly, his wife, was destined a second time to win the conspicuous honour that belongs to a hempen widow.

As his career drew to its appointed close, Fortune withheld her smiles. "People got so peery," complained the great man," that ingenious men were put to dreadful shifts." And then, highest tribute to his greatness, an Act of Parliament was passed which made it a capital offence "for a prig to steal with the hands of other people"; and in the increase of public vigilance his undoing became certain. On the 2nd of January, 1725, a day not easy to forget, a creature of Wild's spoke with fifty yards of lace, worth £40, at his Captain's bidding, and Wild, having otherwise disposed of the plunder, was charged on the 10th of March that he "did feloniously receive of Katharine Stetham ten guineas on account and under colour of helping the said Katharine Stetham to the said lace again, and did not then, nor any time since, discover or apprehend, or cause to be apprehended and brought to Justice, the persons that committed the said felony." Thus runs the indictment, and, to the inexpressible relief of lesser men, Jonathan Wild was condemned to the gallows.

Thereupon he had serious thoughts of "putting his house in order"; with an ironical smile he demanded an explanation of the text: "Cursed is every one that hangeth on a tree"; but, presently reflecting that "his Time was but short in this World, he improved it to the best advantage in Eating, Drinking, Swearing, Cursing, and talking to his Visitants." For all his bragging, drink alone preserved his courage: "he was very restless in the Condemned Hole," though "he gave little or no attention to the condemned Sermon which the purblind Ordinary preached before him," and which was, in Fielding's immortal phrase, "unto the Greeks foolishness." But in the moment of death his distinction returned to him. He tried, but failed, to kill himself; and his progress to the nubbing cheat was a triumph of execration. He reached Tyburn through a howling mob, and died to a yell of universal joy.

The Ordinary has left a record so precious and so lying, that it must needs be quoted at length. The great Thief-Catcher's confession is a masterpiece of comfort, and is so far removed from the truth as completely to justify Fielding's incomparable creation. "Finding there was no room for mercy (and how could I expect mercy, who never showed any)"—thus does the devil-dodger dishonour our Jonathan's memory! —"as soon as I came into the Condemned Hole, I began to think of making a preparation for my soul. . . . To part with my wife, my dear Molly, is so great an Affliction to me, that it touches me to the Quick, and is like Daggers entering into my Heart." How tame the Ordinary's falsehood to the brilliant invention of Fielding, who makes Jonathan kick his Tishy in the very shadow of the Tree! But the Reverend Gentleman gains in unction as he goes. "In the Cart they all kneeled down to prayers and seemed very penitent; the Ordinary used all the means imaginable to make them think of another World, and after singing a penitential Psalm, they cry'd Lord Jesus Christ receive our Souls, the cart drew away and they were all turned off. This is as good an account as can be given by me." Poor Ordinary! If he was modest, he was also untruthful, and you are certain that it was not thus the hero met his death.

Even had Fielding never written his masterpiece, Jonathan Wild would still have been surnamed "The Great." For scarce a chap-book appeared in the year of Jonathan's death that did not expose the only right and true view of his character. "His business," says one hack of prison literature, "at all times was to put a false gloss upon things, and to make fools of mankind." Another precisely formulates the theory of greatness insisted upon by Fielding with so lavish an irony and so masterly a wit. While it is certain that "The History of the Late Mr. Jonathan Wild" is as noble a piece of irony as literature can show, while for the qualities of wit and candour it is equal to its motive, it is likewise true that therein you meet the indubitable Jonathan Wild. It is an entertainment to compare the chap-books of the time with the reasoned, finished work of art: not in any spirit of pedantry—since accuracy in these matters is of small account, but with intent to show how doubly fortunate Fielding was in his genius and in his material. Of course the writer rejoiced in the aid of imagination and eloquence; of course he embellished his picture with such inspirations as Miss Laetitia and the Count; of course he preserves from the first page to the last the highest level of unrivalled irony. But the sketch was there before him, and a lawyer's clerk had treated Jonathan in a vein of heroism within a few weeks of his death. But since a plain statement is never so true as fiction, Fielding's romance is still more credible, still convinces with an easier effort, than the serious and pedestrian records of contemporaries. And you cannot return to its pages without realising that, so far from being "the evolution of a purely intellectual conception," "Jonathan Wild" is a magnificently idealised and ironical portrait of a great man.

III

A PARALLEL

(MOLL CUTPURSE AND JONATHAN WILD)

THEY plied the same trade, each with incomparable success. By her, as by him, the art of the fence was carried to its ultimate perfection. In their hands the high policy of theft wanted nor dignity nor assurance. Neither harboured a single scheme which was not straightway translated into action, and they were masters at once of Newgate and the Highway. As none might rob without the encouragement of his emperor, so none was hanged at Tyburn while intrigue or bribery might avail to drag a half-doomed neck from the halter; and not even Moll herself was more bitterly tyrannical in the control of a reckless gang than the thin-jawed, hatchet-faced Jonathan Wild.

They were statesmen rather than warriors—happy if they might direct the enterprises of others, and determined to punish the lightest disobedience by death. The mind of each was readier than his hand, and neither would risk an easy advantage by a misunderstood or unwonted sleight of hand. But when you leave the exercise of their craft to contemplate their character with a larger eye, it is the woman who at every point has the advantage. Not only was she the peerless inventor of a new cunning; she was at home (and abroad) the better fellow. The suppression of sex was in itself an unparalleled triumph, and the most envious detractor could not but marvel at the domination of her womanhood. Moreover, she shone in a gayer, more splendid epoch. The worthy contemporary of Shakespeare, she had small difficulty in performing feats of prowess and resource which daunted the intrepid ruffians of the eighteenth century. Her period, in brief, gave her an eternal superiority; and it were as hopeless for Otway to surpass the master whom he disgraced, as for Wild to o'ershadow the brilliant example of Moll Cutpurse.

Tyrants both, they exercised their sovereignty in accordance with their varying temperament. Hers was a fine, fat, Falstaffian humour, which, while it inspired Middleton, might have suggested to Shakespeare an equal companion of the drunken knight. His was but a narrow, cynic wit, not edged like the knife, which wellnigh cut his throat, but blunt and scratching like a worn-toothed saw. She laughed with a laugh that echoed from Ludgate to Charing Cross, and her voice drowned all the City. He grinned rarely and with malice ; he piped in a voice shrill and acid as the tricks of his mischievous imagination. She knew no cruelty beyond the necessities of her life, and none regretted more than she the inevitable death of a traitor. He lusted after destruction with a fiendish temper, which was but a grim anticipation of De Sade; he would even smile as he saw the noose tighten round the necks of the poor innocents he had beguiled to Tyburn. It was his boast that he had contrived robberies for the mere glory of dragging his silly victims to the gallows. But Moll, though she stood half-way between the robber and his prey, would have sacrificed a hundred well-earned commissions rather than see her friends and comrades strangled. Her temperament compelled her to the loyal support of her own order, and she would have shrunk in horror from her rival, who, for all his assumed friendship with the thief, was a staunch and subtle ally of justice.

Before all things she had the genius of success. Her public offences were trivial and condoned. She died in her bed, full of years and of honours, beloved by the light-fingered gentry, reverenced by all the judges on the bench. He, for all the sacrifices he made to a squint-eyed law, died execrated alike by populace and police. Already Blueskin had done his worst with a penknife; already Jack Sheppard and his comrades had warned Drury Lane against the infamous thief-catcher. And so anxious, on the other hand, was the law to be quit of their too zealous servant, that an Act of Parliament was passed with the sole object of placing Jonathan's head within the noose. His method, meagre though masterly, lulled him too soon to an impotent security. She, with her larger view of life, her plumper sense of style, was content with nothing less than an ultimate sovereignty, and manifestly did she prove her superiority.

Though born for the wimple, she was more of a man than the breeched and stockinged Jonathan, whose only deed of valiance was to hang, terrier-like, by his teeth to an evasive enemy. While he cheated at cards and cogged the dice, she trained dogs and never missed a bear-baiting. He shrank, like the coward that he was, from the exercise of manly sports; she cared not what were the weapons—quarterstaff or broadsword—so long as she vanquished her opponent. She scoured the town in search of insult; he did but exert his cunning when a quarrel was put upon him. Who, then, shall deny her manhood? Who shall whisper that his style was the braver or the better suited to his sex ?

As became a hero, she kept the best of loose company: her parlour was ever packed with the friends of loyalty and adventure. Are not Hind and Mull Sack worth a thousand Blueskins? Moreover, plunder and wealth were not the only objects of her pursuit: she was not merely a fence but a patriot, and she would have accounted a thousand pounds well lost, if she did but compass the discomfiture of a Parliament-man. Indeed, if Jonathan, the thief-catcher, limped painfully after his magnificent example, Jonathan the man and the sportsman confessed a pitiful inferiority to the valiant Moll. Thus she avenged her sex by distancing the most illustrious of her rivals; and if he pleads for his credit a taste for theology, hers is the chuckle of contemptuous superiority. She died a patriot, bequeathing a fountain of wine to the champions of an exiled king; he died a casuist, setting crabbed problems to the Ordinary. Here, again, the advantage is evident: loyalty is the virtue of men; a sudden attachment to religion is the last resource of the second-rate citizen and of the trapped criminal.

RALPH BRISCOE

A SPARE, lean frame; a small head set forward upon a pair of sloping shoulders; a thin, sharp nose, and rat-like eyes; a flat, hollow chest; shrunk shanks, modestly retreating from their snuff-coloured hose—these are the tokens which served to remind his friends of Ralph Briscoe, the Clerk of Newgate. As he left the prison in the grey air of morning upon some errand of mercy or revenge, he appeared the least fearsome of mortals, while an awkward limp upon his left toe deepened the impression of timidity. So abstract was his manner, so hesitant his gait, that he would hug the wall as he went, nervously stroking its grimy surface with his long, twittering fingers. But Ralph, as justice and the Jug knew too well, was neither fool nor coward. His character belied his outward seeming. A large soul had crept into the case of his wizened body, and if a poltroon among his ancestors had gifted him with an alien type, he had inherited from some nameless warrior both courage and resource.

He was born in easy circumstances, and gently nurtured in the distant village of Kensington. Though cast in a scholar's mould, and very apt for learning, he rebelled from the outset against a career of inaction. His lack of strength was never a check upon his high stomach; he would fight with boys of twice his size, and accept the certain defeat in a cheerful spirit of dogged pugnacity. Moreover, if his arms were weak, his cunning was as keen-edged as his tongue; and, before his stricken eye had paled, he had commonly executed an ample vengeance upon his enemy. Nor was it industry that placed him at the top of the class. A ready wit made him master of the knowledge he despised. But he would always desert his primer to follow the hangman's lumbering cart up Tyburn Hill, and, still a mere imp of mischief, he would run the weary way from Kensington to Shoe Lane on the distant chance of a cock-fight. He was present, so he would relate in after years, when Sir Thomas Jermin's man put his famous trick upon the pit. With a hundred pounds in his pocket and under his arm a dunghill cock, neatly trimmed for the fray, the ingenious ruffian, as Briscoe would tell you, went off to Shoe Lane, persuaded an accomplice to fight the cock in Sir Thomas Jermin's name, and laid a level hundred against his own bird. So lofty was Sir Thomas's repute that backers were easily found, but the dunghill rooster instantly showed a clean pair of heels, and the cheat was justified of his cunning.

Thus Ralph Briscoe learnt the first lessons in that art of sharping wherein he was afterwards an adept; and when he left school his head was packed with many a profitable device which no book learning could impart. His father, however, still resolute that he should join an intelligent profession, sent him to Gray's Inn that he might study law. Here the elegance of his handwriting gained him a rapid repute; his skill became the envy of all the lean-souled clerks in the Inn, and he might have died a respectable attorney had not the instinct of sport forced him from the inkpot and parchment of his profession. Ill could he tolerate the monotony and restraint of this clerkly life. In his eyes law was an instrument, not of justice, but of jugglery. Men were born, said his philosophy, rather to risk their necks than ink their fingers; and if a bold adventure puts you in a difficulty, why, then, you hire some straw-splitting attorney to show his cunning. Indeed, the study of law was for him, as it was for Falstaff, an excuse for many a bout and merry-making. He loved his glass, and he loved his wench, and he loved a bull-baiting better than either. It was his boast, and Moll Cutpurse's compliment, that he never missed a match in his life, and assuredly no man was better known in Paris Garden than the intrepid Ralph Briscoe.

The cloistered seclusion of Gray's Inn grew daily more irksome. There he would sit, in mute despair, drumming the table with his fingers, and biting the quill, whose use he so bitterly contemned. Of winter afternoons he would stare through the leaded window-panes at the gaunt, leafless trees, on whose summits swayed the cawing rooks, until servitude seemed intolerable, and he prayed for the voice of the bear-ward that summoned him to Southwark. And when the chained bear, the familiar monkey on his back, followed the shrill bagpipe along the curious street, Briscoe felt that blood, not ink, coursed in his veins, forgot the tiresome impediment of the law, and joined the throng, hungry for this sport of kings. Nor was he the patron of an enterprise wherein he dared take no part. He was as bold and venturesome as the bravest ruffler that ever backed a dog at a baiting. When the bull, cruelly secured behind, met the onslaught of his opponents, throwing them off, now this side, now that, with his horns, Briscoe, lost in excitement, would leap into the ring that not a point of the combat should escape him.

So it was that he won the friendship of his illustrious benefactress, Moll Cutpurse. For, one day, when he had ventured too near the maddened bull, the brute made a heave at his breeches, which instantly gave way; and in another moment he would have been gored to death, had not Moll seized him by the collar and slung him out of the ring. Thus did his courage ever contradict his appearance, and at the dangerous game of whipping the blinded bear he had no rival, either for bravery or adroitness. He would rush in with uplifted whip until the breath of the infuriated beast was hot upon his cheek, let his angry lash curl for an instant across the bear's flank, and then, for all his halting foot, leap back into safety with a smiling pride in his own nimbleness.

His acquaintance with Moll Cutpurse, casually begun at a bull-baiting, speedily ripened, for her into friendship, for him into love. In this, the solitary romance of his life, Ralph Briscoe overtopped even his own achievements of courage. The Roaring Girl was no more young, and years had not refined her character unto gentleness. It was still her habit to appear publicly in jerkin and galligaskins, to smoke tobacco in contempt of her sex, and to fight her enemies with a very fury of insolence. In stature she exceeded the limping clerk by a head, and she could pick him up with one hand, like a kitten. Yet he loved her, not for any grace of person, nor beauty of feature, nor even because her temperament was undaunted as his own. He loved her for that wisest of reasons, which is no reason at all, because he loved her. In his eyes she was the Queen, not of Misrule, but of Hearts. Had a throne been his, she should have shared it, and he wooed her with a shy intensity, which ennobled him, even in her austere regard. Alas! she was unable to return his passion, and she lamented her own obduracy with characteristic humour. She made no attempt to conceal her admiration. "A notable and famous person," she called him, confessing that, "he was right for her tooth, and made to her mind in every part of him." He had been bred up in the same exercise of bull-baiting, which was her own delight; she had always praised his towardliness, and prophesied his preferment. But when he paid her court she was obliged to decline the honour, while she esteemed the compliment. In truth, she was completely insensible to passion, or, as she exclaimed in a phrase of brilliant independence, "I should have hired him to my embraces."

The sole possibility that remained was a Platonic friendship, and Briscoe accepted the situation in excellent humour. "Ever since he came to know himself," again it is Moll that speaks, "he always deported himself to me with an abundance of regard, calling me his Aunt." And his aunt she remained unto the end, bound to him in a proper and natural alliance. Different as they were in aspect, they were strangely alike in taste and disposition. Nor was the Paris Garden their only meeting ground. His sorry sojourn in Gray's Inn had thrown him on the side of the lawbreaker, and he had acquired a strange cunning in the difficult art of evading justice. Instantly Moll recognised his practical value, and, exerting all her talent for intrigue, presently secured for him the Clerkship of Newgate. Here at last he found scope not only for his learning, but for that spirit of adventure that breathed within him. His meagre acquaintance with letters placed him on a pinnacle high above his colleagues. Now and then a prisoner proved his equal in wit, but as he was manifestly superior in intelligence to the Governor, the Ordinary, and all the warders, he speedily seized and hereafter retained the real sovereignty of Newgate.

His early progress was barred by envy and contempt. Why, asked the men in possession, should this shrivelled stranger filch our privileges? But Briscoe met their malice with an easy smile, knowing that at all points he was more than their match. His alliance with Moll stood him in good stead, and in a few months the twain were the supreme arbiters of English justice. Should a highwayman seek to save his neck, he must first pay a fat indemnity to the Newgate Clerk, but, since Moll was the appointed banker of the whole family, she was quick to sanction whatever price her accomplice suggested. And Briscoe had a hundred other tricks whereby he increased his riches and repute. There was no debtor came to Newgate whom the Clerk would not aid, if he believed the kindness profitable. Suppose his inquiries gave an assurance of his victim's recovery, he would house him comfortably, feed him at his own table, lend him money, and even condescend to win back the generous loan by the dice-box.

His civility gave him a general popularity among the prisoners, and his appearance in the Yard was a signal for a subdued hilarity. He drank and gambled with the roysterers; he babbled a cheap philosophy with the erudite; and he sold the necks of all to the highest bidder. Though now and again he was convicted of mercy or revenge, he commonly held himself aloof from human passions, and pursued the one sane end of life in an easy security. The hostility of his colleagues irked him but little. A few tags of Latin, the friendship of Moll, and a casual threat of exposure frightened the Governor into acquiescence, but the Ordinary was more difficult of conciliation. The Clerk had not been long in Newgate before he saw that between the reverend gentleman and himself there could be naught save war. Hitherto the Ordinary had reserved to his own profit the right of intrigue; he it was who had received the hard-scraped money of the sorrowing relatives, and untied the noose when it seemed good to him. But Briscoe insisted upon a division of labour. "It is your business," he said, "to save the scoundrels in the other world. Leave to me the profit of their salvation in this." And the Clerk triumphed after his wont: freedom jingled in his pocket; he doled out comfort, even life, to the oppressed; and he extorted a comfortable fortune in return for privileges which were never in his gift.

Without the walls of Newgate the house of his frequentation was the "Dog Tavern." Thither he would wander every afternoon to meet his clients and to extort blood-money. In this haunt of criminals and pettifoggers no man was better received than the Newgate Clerk, and while he assumed a manner of generous cordiality, it was a strange sight to see him wince when some sturdy ruffian slapped him too strenuously upon the back. He had a joke and a chuckle for all, and his merry quips, dry as they were, were joyously quoted to all new-comers. His legal ingenuity appeared miraculous, and it was confidently asserted in the Coffee House that he could turn black to white with so persuasive an argument that there was no Judge on the Bench to confute him. But he was not omnipotent, and his zeal encountered many a serious check. At times he failed to save the necks even of his intimates, since when once a ruffian was notorious, Moll and the Clerk fought vainly for his release. Thus it was that Cheney, the famous wrestler, whom Ralph had often backed against all comers, died at Tyburn. He had been taken by the troopers red-handed upon the highway. Seized after a desperate resistance, he was wounded well-nigh to death, and Briscoe quoted a dozen precedents to prove that he was unfit to be tried or hanged. Argument failing, the munificent Clerk offered fifty pounds for the life of his friend. But to no purpose: the valiant wrestler was carried to the cart in a chair, and so lifted to the gallows, which cured him of his gaping wounds.

When the Commonwealth administered justice with pedantic severity, Briscoe's influence still further declined. There was no longer scope in the State for men of spirit; even the gaols were handed over to the stern mercy of crop-eared Puritans; Moll herself had fallen upon evil times; and Ralph Briscoe determined to make a last effort for wealth and retirement. At the very moment when his expulsion seemed certain, an heiress was thrown into Newgate upon a charge of murdering a too importunate suitor. The chain of evidence was complete: the dagger plunged in his heart was recognised for her own; she was seen to decoy him to the secret corner of a wood, where his raucous love-making was silenced for ever. Taken off her guard, she had even hinted confession of her crime, and nothing but intrigue could have saved her gentle neck from the gallows. Briscoe, hungry for her money-bags, promised assistance. He bribed, he threatened, he cajoled, he twisted the law as only he could twist it, he suppressed honest testimony, he procured false; in fine, he weakened the case against her with so resistless an effrontery, that not the Hanging Judge himself could convict the poor innocent.

At the outset he had agreed to accept a handsome bribe, but as the trial approached, his avarice increased, and he would be content with nothing less than the lady's hand and fortune. Not that he loved her; his heart was long since given to Moll Cutpurse; but he knew that his career of depredation was at an end, and it became him to provide for his declining years. The victim repulsed his suit, regretting a thousand times that she had stabbed her ancient lover. But, at last, bidden summarily to choose between Death and the Clerk, she chose the Clerk, and thus Ralph Briscoe left Newgate the richest squire in a western county. Henceforth he farmed his land like a gentleman, drank with those of his neighbours who would crack a bottle with him, and unlocked the strange stores of his memory to bumpkins who knew not the name of Newgate. Still devoted to sport, he hunted the fox, and made such a bull-ring as his youthful imagination could never have pictured. So he lived a life of country ease, and died a churchwarden. And he deserved his prosperity, for he carried the soul of Falstaff in the shrunken body of Justice Shallow.

GILDEROY AND SIXTEEN-STRING JACK
I
GILDEROY

HE stood six feet ten in his stockinged feet, and was the tallest ruffian that ever cut a purse or held up a coach on the highway. A mass of black hair curled over a low forehead, and a glittering eye intensified his villainous aspect; nor did a deep scar, furrowing his cheek from end to end, soften the horror of his sudden apparition. Valiant men shuddered at his approach; women shrank from the distant echo of his name; for fifteen years he terrorised Scotland from Caithness to the border; and the most partial chronicler never insulted his memory with the record of a good deed.

He was born to a gentle family in the Calendar of Monteith, and was celebrated even in boyhood for his feats of strength and daring. While still at school he could hold a hundredweight at arm's-length, and crumple up a horseshoe like a wisp of hay. The fleetest runner, the most desperate fighter in the country, he was already famous before his name was besmirched with crime, and he might have been immortalised as the Hercules of the seventeenth century, had not his ambition been otherwise flattered. At the outset, though the inclination was never lacking, he knew small temptation to break the sterner laws of conduct. His pleasures were abundantly supplied by his father's generosity, and he had no need to refrain from such vices as became a gentleman. If he was no drunkard, it was because his head was equal to the severest strain, and, despite his forbidding expression, he was always a successful breaker of hearts. His very masterfulness overcame the most stubborn resistance; and more than once the pressure of his dishonourable suit converted hatred into love. At the very time that he was denounced for Scotland's disgrace, his praises were chanted in many a dejected ballad. "Gilderoy was a bonny boy," sang one heart-broken maiden:

Had roses till his shoon, His stockings were of silken soy, Wi' garters hanging doon.

But in truth he was admired less for his amiability than for that quality of governance which, when once he had torn the decalogue to pieces, made him a veritable emperor of crime.

His father's death was the true beginning of his career. A modest patrimony was squandered in six months, and Gilderoy had no penny left wherewith to satisfy the vices which insisted upon indulgence. He demanded money at all hazards, and money without toil. For a while his more clamant needs were fulfilled by the amiable simplicity of his mother, whom he blackmailed with insolence and contempt. And when she, wearied by his shameless importunity, at last withdrew her support, he determined upon a monstrous act of vengeance. With a noble affectation of penitence he visited his home; promised reform at supper; and said good-night in the broken accent of reconciliation. But no sooner was the house sunk in slumber than he crawled stealthily upstairs in order to forestall by theft a promised generosity. He opened the door of the bed-chamber in a hushed silence; but the wrenching of the coffer-lid awoke the sleeper, and Gilderoy, having cut his mother's throat with an infamous levity, seized whatever money and jewels were in the house, cruelly maltreated his sister, and laughingly burnt the house to the ground, that the possibility of evidence might be destroyed.

Henceforth his method of plunder was assured. It was part of his philosophy to prevent detection by murder, and the flames from the burning walls added a pleasure to his lustful eye. His march across Scotland was marked by slaughtered families and ruined houses. Plunder was the first cause of his exploits, but there is no doubt that death and arson were a solace to his fierce spirit; and for a while this giant of cruelty knew neither check nor hindrance. Presently it became a superstition with him that death was the inevitable accompaniment of robbery, and, as he was incapable of remorse, he grew callous, and neglected the simplest precautions. At Dunkeld he razed a rifled house to the ground, and with the utmost effrontery repeated the performance at Aberdeen. But at last he had been tracked by a company of soldiers, who, that justice might not be cheated of her prey, carried him to gaol, where after the briefest trial he was condemned to death.

Gilderoy, however, was still master of himself. His immense strength not only burst his bonds, but broke prison, and this invincible Samson was once more free in Aberdeen, inspiring that respectable city with a legendary dread. The reward of one hundred pounds was offered in vain. Had he shown himself on the road in broad daylight, none would have dared to arrest him, and it was not until his plans were deliberately laid, that he crossed the sea. The more violent period of his career was at an end. Never again did he yield to his passion for burning and sudden death; and, if the world found him unconquerable, his self-control is proved by the fact that in the heyday of his strength he turned from his unredeemed brutality to a gentler method. He now deserted Scotland for France, with which, like all his countrymen, he claimed a cousin-ship; and so profoundly did he impose upon Paris with his immense stature, his elegant attire, his courtly manners (for he was courtesy itself, when it pleased him), that he was taken for an eminent scholar, or at least a soldier of fortune.

Prosperity might doubtless have followed a discreet profession, but Gilderoy must still be thieving, and he reaped a rich harvest among the unsuspicious courtiers of France. His most highly renowned exploit was performed at St. Denis, and the record of France's humiliation is still treasured. The great church was packed with ladies of fashion and their devout admirers. Richelieu attended in state; the king himself shone upon the assembly. The strange Scotsman, whom no man knew and all men wondered at, attracted a hundred eyes to himself and his magnificent equipment. But it was not his to be idle, and at the very moment whereat Mass was being sung, he contrived to lighten Richelieu's pocket of a purse. The king was a delighted witness of the theft; but Gilderoy, assuming an air of facile intimacy, motioned him to silence; and he, deeming it a trick put upon Richelieu by a friend, hastened, at the service-end, to ask his minister if perchance he had a purse of gold upon him. Richelieu instantly discovered the loss, to the king's uncontrolled hilarity, which was mitigated when it was found that the thief, having emptied the king's pocket at the unguarded moment of his merriment, had left them both the poorer.

Such were Gilderoy's interludes of gaiety; and when you remember the cynical ferocity of his earlier performance, you cannot deny him the credit of versatility. He stayed in France until his ominous reputation was too widely spread; whereupon he crossed the Pyrenees, travelling like a gentleman, in a brilliant carriage of his own. From Spain he carried off a priceless collection of silver plate; and he returned to his own country, fatigued, yet unsoftened, by the grand tour. Meanwhile, a forgetful generation had not kept his memory green. The monster, who punished Scotland a year ago with fire and sword, had passed into oblivion, and Gilderoy was able to establish for himself a new reputation. He departed as far as possible from his ancient custom, joined the many cavaliers, who were riding up and down the country, pistol in hand, and presently proved a dauntless highwayman. He had not long ridden in the neighbourhood of Perth before he met the Earl of Linlithgow, from whom he took a gold watch, a diamond ring, and eighty guineas. Being an outlaw, he naturally espoused the King's cause, and would have given a year of his life to meet a Regicide. Once upon a time, says rumour, he found himself face to face with Oliver Cromwell, whom he dragged from his coach, set ignominiously upon an ass, and so turned adrift with his feet tied under the beast's belly. But the story is incredible, not only because the loyal historians of the time caused Oliver to be robbed daily on every road in Great Britain, but because our Gilderoy, had he ever confronted the Protector, most assuredly would not have allowed him to escape with his life.

Tired of scouring the highway, Gilderoy resolved upon another enterprise. He collected a band of fearless ruffians, and placed himself at their head. With this army to aid, he harried Sutherland and the North, lifting cattle, plundering homesteads, and stopping wayfarers with a humour and adroitness worthy of Robin Hood. No longer a lawless adventurer, he made his own conditions of life, and forced the people to obey them. He who would pay Gilderoy a fair contribution ran no risk of losing his sheep or oxen. But evasion was impossible, and the smallest suspicion of falsehood was punished by death. The peaceably inclined paid their toll with regret; the more daring opposed the raider to their miserable undoing; the timid satisfied the utmost exactions of Gilderoy, and deemed themselves fortunate if they left the country with their lives.

Thus Scotland became a land of dread; the most restless man within her borders hardly dare travel beyond his byre. The law was powerless against this indomitable scourge, and the reward of a thousand marks would have been offered in vain, had not Gilderoy's cruelty estranged his mistress. This traitress—Peg Cunningham was her name—less for avarice than in revenge for many insults and infidelities, at last betrayed her master. Having decoyed him to her house, she admitted fifty armed men, and thus imagined a full atonement for her unnumbered wrongs. But Gilderoy was triumphant to the last. Instantly suspecting the treachery of his mistress, he burst into her bed-chamber, and, that she might not enjoy the price of blood, ripped her up with a hanger. Then he turned defiant upon the army arrayed against him, and killed eight men before the others captured him. Disarmed after a desperate struggle, he was loaded with chains and carried to Edinburgh, where he was starved for three days, and then hanged without the formality of a trial on a gibbet, thirty feet high, set up in the Grassmarket. But even then Scotland's vengeance was unsatisfied. The body, cut down from its first gibbet, was hung in chains forty feet above Leith Walk, where it creaked and gibbered as a warning to evildoers for half a century, until at last the inhabitants of that respectable quarter petitioned that Gilderoy's bones should cease to rattle, and that they should enjoy the peace impossible for his jingling skeleton.

Gilderoy was no drawing-room scoundrel, no villain of schoolgirl romance. He felt remorse as little as he felt fear, and there was no crime from whose commission he shrank. Before his death he confessed to thirty-seven murders, and bragged that he had long since lost count of his robberies and rapes. Something must be abated for boastfulness. But after all deduction there remains a tale of crime that is unsurpassed. His most admirably artistic quality is his complete consistence. He was a ruffian finished and rotund; he made no concession, be betrayed no weakness. Though he never preached a sermon against the human race, he practised a brutality which might have proceeded from a gospel of hate. He spared neither friends nor relatives, and he murdered his own mother with as light a heart as he sent a strange widow of Aberdeen to her death. His skill is undoubted, and he proved by the discipline of his band that he was not without some talent of generalship. But he owed much of his success to his physical strength, and to the temperament, which never knew the scandal of hesitancy or dread.

A born marauder, he devoted his life to his trade; and, despite his travels in France and Spain, he enjoyed few intervals of merriment. Even the humour, which proved his redemption, was as dour and grim as Scotland can furnish at her grimmest and dourest Here is a specimen will serve as well as another: three of Gilderoy's gang had been hanged according to the sentence of a certain Lord of Session, and the Chieftain, for his own vengeance and the intimidation of justice, resolved upon an exemplary punishment. He waylaid the Lord of Session, emptied his pockets, killed his horses, broke his coach in pieces, and having bound his lackeys drowned them in a pond. This was but the prelude of revenge, for presently (and here is the touch of humour) he made him ride at dead of night to the gallows, whereon the three malefactors were hanging. One arm of the crossbeams was still untenanted. "But my soul, mon," cried Gilderoy to the Lord of Session, "as this gibbet is built to break people's craigs, and is not uniform without another, I must e'en hang you upon the vacant beam." And straightway the Lord of Session swung in the moon-light, and Gilderoy had cracked his black and solemn joke.

But this sense of fun is the single trait which relieves the colossal turpitude of Gilderoy. And, though even his turpitude was melodramatic in its lack of balance, it is this unity of character which is the foundation of his greatness. He was no fum-bler, led away from his purpose by the first diversion; his ambition was clear before him, and he never fell below it. He defied Scotland for fifteen years, was hanged so high that he passed into a proverb, and though his handsome, sinister face might have made women his slaves, he was never betrayed by passion (or by virtue) to an amiability.

II
SIXTEEN-STRING JACK

THE "Green Pig" stood in the solitude of the North Road. Its simple front, its neatly balanced windows, curtained with white, gave it an air of comfort and tran-quillity. The smoke which curled from its hospitable chimney spoke of warmth and good fare. To pass it was to spurn the last chance of a bottle for many a weary mile, and the prudent traveller would always rest an hour by its ample fireside, or gossip with its fantastic hostess. Now, the hostess of the little inn was Ellen Roach, friend and accomplice of Sixteen-String Jack, once the most famous woman in England, and still after a weary stretch at Botany Bay the strangest of companions, the most buxom of spinsters. Her beauty was elusive even in her triumphant youth, and middle-age had neither softened her traits nor refined her expression. Her auburn hair, once the glory of Covent Garden, was fading to a withered grey; she was never tall enough to endure an encroaching stoutness with equanimity; her dumpy figure made you marvel at her past success; and hardship had furrowed her candid brow into wrinkles. But when she opened her lips she became instantly animated. With a glass before her on the table, she would prattle frankly and engagingly of the past. Strange cities had she seen; she had faced the dangers of an adventurous life with calmness and good temper. And yet Botany Bay, with its attendant horrors, was already fading from her memory. In imagination she was still with her incomparable hero, and it was her solace, after fifteen years, to sing the praise and echo the perfections of Sixteen-String Jack.

"How well I remember," she would murmur, as though unconscious of her audience, "the unhappy day when Jack Rann was first arrested. It was May, and he came back travel-stained and weary in the brilliant dawn. He had stopped a one-horse shay near the nine-mile stone on the Hounslow Road—every word of his confession is burnt into my brain—and had taken a watch and a handful of guineas. I was glad enough of the money, for there was no penny in the house, and presently I sent the maid-servant to make the best bargain she could with the watch. But the silly jade, by the saddest of mishaps, took the trinket straight to the very man who made it, and he, suspecting a theft, had us both arrested. Even then Jack might have been safe, had not the devil prompted me to speak the truth. Dismayed by the magistrate, I owned, wretched woman that I was, that I had received the watch from Rann, and in two hours Jack also was under lock and key. Yet, when we were sent for trial I made what amends I could. I declared on oath that I had never seen Sixteen-String Jack in my life; his name came to my lips by accident; and, hector as they would, the lawyers could not frighten me to an acknowledgment. Meanwhile Jack's own behaviour was superb. I was the proudest woman in England as I stood by his side in the dock. When you compared him with Sir John Fielding, you did not doubt for an instant which was the finer gentleman. And what a dandy was my Jack! Though he came there to answer for his life, he was all ribbons and furbelows. His irons were tied up with the daintiest blue bows, and in the breast of his coat he carried a bundle of flowers as large as a birch-broom. His neck quivered in the noose, yet he was never cowed to civility. 'I know no more of the matter than you do,' he

cried indignantly, 'nor half so much neither,' and if the magistrate had not been
an ill-mannered oaf, he would not have dared to disbelieve my true-hearted Jack.
That time we escaped with whole skins; and off we went, after dinner, to Vauxhall,
where Jack was more noticed than the fiercest of the bloods, and where he filled the
heart of George Barrington with envy. Nor was he idle, despite his recent escape:
he brought away two watches and three purses from the Garden, so that our necessities were amply supplied. Ah, I should have been happy in those days if only Jack
had been faithful. But he had a roving eye and a joyous temperament; and though
he loved me better than any of the baggages to whom he paid court, he would not
visit me so often as he should. Why, once he was hustled off to Bow Street because
the watch caught him climbing in at Doll Frampton's window. And she, the shameless minx, got him off by declaring in open court that she would be proud to receive
him whenever he would deign to ring at her bell. But that is the penalty of loving a
great man: you must needs share his affection with a set of unworthy wenches. Yet
Jack was always kind to me, and I was the chosen companion of his pranks.

"Never can I forget the splendid figure he cut that day at Bagnigge Wells. We
had driven down in our coach, and all the world marvelled at our magnificence.
Jack was brave in a scarlet coat, a tambour waistcoat, and white silk stockings. From
the knees of his breeches streamed the strings (eight at each), whence he got his
name, and as he plucked off his lace-hat the dinner-table rose at him. That was a
moment worth living for, and when, after his first bottle, Jack rattled the glasses, and declared himself a highwayman, the whole company shuddered. 'But, my
friends,' quoth he, 'to-day I am making holiday, so that you have naught to fear.'
When the wine's in, the wit's out, and Jack could never stay his hand from the
bottle. The more he drank, the more he bragged, until, thoroughly fuddled, he
lost a ring from his finger, and charged the miscreants in the room with stealing it.
'However,' hiccupped he, ''tis a mere nothing, worth a paltry hundred pounds—less
than a lazy evening's work. So I'll let the trifling theft pass.' But the cowards were
not content with Jack's generosity, and seizing upon him, they thrust him neck and
crop through the window. They were seventeen to one, the craven-hearted loons;
and I could but leave the marks of my nails on the cheek of the foremost, and follow my hero into the yard, where we took coach, and drove sulkily back to Covent
Garden.

"And yet he was not always in a mad humour; in fact, Sixteen-String Jack, for all his gaiety, was a proud, melancholy man. The shadow of the tree was always upon him, and he would make me miserable by talking of his certain doom. 'I have a hundred pounds in my pocket,' he would say; 'I shall spend that, and then I sha'n't last long.' And though I never thought him serious, his prophecy came true enough. Only a few months before the end we had visited Tyburn together. With his usual carelessness, he passed the line of constables who were on guard. 'It is very proper,' said he, in his jauntiest tone, 'that I should be a spectator on this melancholy occasion.' And though none of the dullards took his jest, they instantly made way for him. For my Jack was always a gentleman, though he was bred to the stable, and his bitterest enemy could not have denied that he was handsome. His open countenance was as honest as the day, and the brown curls over his forehead were more elegant than the smartest wig. Wherever he went the world did him honour, and many a time my vanity was sorely wounded. I was a pretty girl, mind you, though my travels have not improved my beauty; and I had many admirers before ever I picked up Jack Rann at a masquerade. Why, there was a Templar, with two thousand a year, who gave me a carriage and servants while I still lived at the dressmaker's in Oxford Street, and I was not out of my teens when the old Jew in St. Mary Axe took me into keeping. But when Jack was by, I had no chance of admiration. All the eyes were glued upon him, and his poor doxy had to be content with a furtive look thrown over a stranger's shoulder. At Barnet races, the year before they sent me across the sea, we were followed by a crowd the livelong day; and truly Jack, in his blue satin waistcoat laced with silver, might have been a peer. At any rate, he had not his equal on the course, and it is small wonder that never for a moment were we left to ourselves.

"But happiness does not last for ever; only too often we were pinched for money, and Jack, finding his purse empty, could do naught else than hire a hackney and take to the road again, while I used to lie awake listening to the watchman's raucous voice, and praying God to send back my warrior rich and scathless. So times grew more and more difficult. Jack would stay a whole night upon the heath, and come home with an empty pocket or a beggarly half-crown. And there was nothing, after a shabby coat, that he hated half so much as a sheriff's officer. 'Learn a lesson in politeness,' he said to one of the wretches who dragged him off to the Marshalsea.

'When Sir John Fielding's people come after me they use me genteelly; they only hold up a finger, beckon me, and I follow as quietly as a lamb. But you bluster and insult, as though you had never dealings with gentlemen.' Poor Jack, he was of a proud stomach, and could not abide interference; yet they would never let him go free. And he would have been so happy had he been allowed his own way. To pull out a rusty pistol now and again, and to take a purse from a traveller—surely these were innocent pleasures, and he never meant to hurt a fellow-creature. But for all his kindness of heart, for all his love of splendour and fine clothes, they took him at last.

"And this time, too, it was a watch which was our ruin. How often did I warn him: 'Jack,' I would say, 'take all the money you can. Guineas tell no tale. But leave the watches in their owners' fobs.' Alas! he did not heed my words, and the last man he ever stopped on the road was that pompous rascal, Dr. Bell, then chaplain to the Princess Amelia. 'Give me your money,' screamed Jack, 'and take no notice or I'll blow your brains out.' And the doctor gave him all that he had, the mean-spirited devil-dodger, and it was no more than eighteenpence. Now what should a man of courage do with eighteenpence? So poor Jack was forced to seize the parson's watch and trinkets as well, and thus it was that we stood a second time at the Old Bailey. When Jack brought home the watch, I was seized with a shuddering presentiment, and I would have given the world to throw it out of the window. But I could not bear to see him pinched with hunger, and he had already tossed the doctor's eighteenpence to a beggar woman. So I trudged off to the pawnbroker's, to get what price I could, and I bethought me that none would know me for what I was so far away as Oxford Street. But the monster behind the counter entertained an instant suspicion, though I swear I looked as innocent as a babe; he discovered the owner of the watch, and infamously followed me to my house.

"The next day we were both arrested, and once more we stood in the hot, stifling Court of the Old Bailey. Jack was radiant as ever, the one spot of colour and gaiety in that close, sodden atmosphere. When we were taken from Bow Street a thousand people formed our guard of honour, and for a month we were the twin wonders of London. The lightest word, the fleetest smile of the renowned highwayman, threw the world into a fit of excitement, and a glimpse of Rann was worth a king's ransom. And I could look upon him all day for nothing! And I knew what a fever of apprehension throbbed behind his mask of happy contempt. Yet bravely he played the part unto the very end. If the toasts of London were determined to gaze at him, he assured them they should have a proper salve for their eyes. And so he dressed himself as a lighthearted sportsman. His coat and waistcoat were of pea-green cloth; his buckskin breeches were spotlessly new, and all tricked out with the famous strings; his hat was bound round with silver cords; and even the ushers of the Court were touched to courtesy. He would whisper to me, as we stood in the dock, 'Cheer up, my girl. I have ordered the best supper that Covent Garden can provide, and we will make merry to-night when this foolish old judge has done his duty.' But the supper was never eaten. Through the weary afternoon we waited for acquittal. The autumn sun sank in hopeless gloom. The wretched lamps twinkled through the jaded air of the court-house. In an hour I lived a thousand years of misery, and when the sentence was read, the words carried no sense to my withered brain. It was only in my cell I realised that I had seen Jack Rann for the last time; that his pea-green coat would prove a final and ineffaceable memory.

"Alas! I, who had never been married, was already a hempen widow; but I was too hopelessly heartbroken for my lover's fate to think of my own paltry hardship. I never saw him again. They told me that he suffered at Tyburn like a man, and that he counted upon a rescue to the very end. They told me (still bitterer news to hear) that two days before his death he entertained seven women at supper, and was in the wildest humour. This almost broke my heart; it was an infidelity committed on the other side of the grave. But, poor Jack, he was a good lad, and loved me more than them all, though he never could be faithful to me." And thus, bidding the drawer bring fresh glasses, Ellen Roach would end her story. Though she had told it a hundred times, at the last words a tear always sparkled in her eye. She lived without friend and without lover, faithful to the memory of Sixteen-String Jack, who for her was the only reality in a world of shades. Her middle-age was as distant as her youth. The dressmaker's in Oxford Street was as vague a dream as the inhospitable shore of Botany Bay. So she waited on to a weary eld, proud of the "Green Pig's" well-ordered comfort, prouder still that for two years she shared the glory of Jack Rann, and that she did not desert her hero, even in his punishment.

III
A PARALLEL

(GILDEROY AND SIXTEEN-STRING JACK)

THEIR closest parallel is the notoriety which dogged them from the very day of their death. Each, for his own exploits, was the most famous man of his time, the favourite of broadsheets, the prime hero of the ballad-mongers. And each owed his fame as much to good fortune as to merit, since both were excelled in their generation by more skilful scoundrels. If Gilderoy was unsurpassed in brutality, he fell immeasurably below Hind in artistry and wit, nor may he be compared to such accomplished highwaymen as Mull Sack or the Golden Farmer. His method was not elevated by a touch of the grand style. He stamped all the rules of the road beneath his contemptuous foot, and cared not what enormity he committed in his quest for gold. Yet, though he lived in the true Augustan age, he yielded to no one of his rivals in glorious recognition. So, too, Jack Rann, of the Sixteen Strings, was a near contemporary of George Barrington. While that nimble-fingered prig was making a brilliant appearance at Vauxhall, and emptying the pockets of his intimates, Rann was riding over Hounslow Heath, and flashing his pistol in the eye of the wayfarer. The very year in which Jack danced his last jig at Tyburn, Barrington had astonished London by a fruitless attempt to steal Prince Orloff's miraculous snuff-box. And not even Ellen Roach herself would have dared to assert that Rann was Barrington's equal in sleight of hand. But Rann holds his own against the best of his craft, with an imperishable name, while a host of more distinguished cracksmen are excluded even from the Newgate Calendar.

But, in truth, there is one quality which has naught to do with artistic supremacy; and in this quality both Rann and Gilderoy were rich beyond their fellows. They knew (none better) how to impose upon the world. Had their deserts been even less than they were, they would still have been bravely notorious. It is a common superstition that the talent for advertisement has but a transitory effect, that time sets all men in their proper places. Nothing can be more false; for he who has once declared himself among the great ones of the earth, not only holds his position while he lives, but forces an unreasoning admiration upon the future. He declines from the lofty throne, whereon his own vanity and love of praise have set him, but he still stands above the modest level which contents the genuinely great. Why does Euripides still throw a shadow upon the worthier poets of his time? Because he had the faculty of displacement, because he could compel the world to profess an interest not only in his work but in himself. Why is Michael Angelo a loftier figure in the history of art than Donatello, the supreme sculptor of his time? Because Donatello had not the temper which would bully a hundred popes, and extract a magnificent advertisement from each encounter. Why does Shelley still claim a larger share of the world's admiration than Keats, his indubitable superior? Because Shelley was blessed or cursed with the trick of interesting the world by a side issue.

So by a similar faculty Gilderoy and Jack Rann have kept themselves and their achievements in the light of day. Had they lived in the nineteenth century they might have been the vendors of patent pills, or the chairmen of bubble companies. But whatever trade they had followed, their names would have been on every hoarding, their wares would have been puffed in every journal. They understood the art of publicity better than any of their contemporaries, and they are remembered not because they were the best thieves of their time, but because they were determined to interest the people in their misdeeds. Gilderoy's brutality, which was always theatrical, ensured a constant remembrance, and the lofty gallows added to his repute; while the brilliant inspiration of the strings which decorated Rann's breeches, was sufficient to conquer death. How should a hero sink to oblivion who had chosen for himself so splendid a name as Sixteen-String Jack?

So far, then, their achievement is parallel. And parallel also is their taste for melodrama. Each employed means too great or too violent for the end in view. Gilderoy burnt houses and ravished women, when his sole object was the acquisition of money. Sixteen-String Jack terrified Bagnigge Wells with the dreadful announcement that he was a highwayman, when his kindly, stupid heart would have shrunk from the shedding of a drop of blood. So they both blustered through the world, the one in deed, the other in word; and both played their parts with so little refinement that they frightened the groundlings to a timid admiration. But here the resemblance is at an end. In the essentials of their trade Gilderoy was a professional, Rann a mere amateur. They both bullied; but, while Sixteen-String Jack was content to shout threats, and pick up half-a-crown, Gilderoy breathed murder, and demanded a vast ransom. Only once in his career did the "disgraceful Scotsman" become gay and debonair. Only once did he relax the tension of his frown, and pick pockets with the lightness and freedom of a gentleman. It was on his voyage to France that he forgot his old policy of arson and pillage, and truly the Court of the Great King was not the place for his rapacious cruelty. Jack Rann, on the other hand, would have taken life as a prolonged jest, if Sir John Fielding and the sheriffs had not checked his mirth. He was but a bungler on the road, with no more resource than he might have learned from the common chap-book, or from the dying speeches, hawked in Newgate Street. But he had a fine talent for merriment; he loved nothing so well as a smart coat and a pretty woman. Thieving was no passion with him, but a necessity. How could he dance at a masquerade or court his Ellen with an empty pocket? So he took to the road as the sole profession of an idle man, and he bullied his way from Hounslow to Epping in sheer lightness of heart. After all, to rob Dr. Bell of eighteenpence was the work of a simpleton. But it was a very pretty taste which expressed itself in a pea-green coat and deathless strings; and Rann will keep posterity's respect rather for the accessories of his art than for the art itself. On the other hand, you cannot imagine Gilderoy habited otherwise than in black; you cannot imagine this monstrous matricide taking pleasure in the smaller elegancies of life. From first to last he was the stern and beetle-browed marauder, who would have despised the frippery of Sixteen-String Jack as vehemently as his sudden appearance would have frightened the foppish lover of Ellen Roach.

Their conduct with women is sufficient index of their character. Jack Rann was too general a lover for fidelity. But he was amiable, even in his unfaithfulness; he won the undying affection of his Ellen; he never stood in the dock without a nosegay tied up by fair and nimble fingers; he was attended to Tyburn by a bevy of distinguished admirers. Gilderoy, on the other hand, approached women in a spirit of violence. His Sadie temper drove him to kill those whom he affected to love. And his cruelty was amply repaid. While Ellen Roach perjured herself to save the lover, to whose memory she professed a life-long loyalty, it was Peg Cunningham who wreaked her vengeance in the betrayal of Gilderoy. He remained true to his character, when he ripped up the belly of his betrayer. This was the closing act of his life. Rann, also, was consistent, even to the gallows. The night before his death he entertained seven women at supper, and out-laughed them all. But the contrast is not so violent as it appears. The one act is melodrama, the other farce. And what is farce, but melodrama in a happier shape?

THOMAS PURENEY

THOMAS PURENEY, Archbishop among Ordinaries, lived and preached in the heyday of Newgate. His was the good fortune to witness Sheppard's encounter with the topsman, and to shrive the battered soul of Jonathan Wild. Nor did he fall one inch below his opportunity. Designed by Providence to administer a final consolation to the evildoer, he permitted no false ambition to distract his talent. As some men are born for the gallows, so he was born to thump the cushion of a prison pulpit; and his peculiar aptitude was revealed to him before he had time to spend his strength in mistaken endeavour.

For thirty years his squat, stout figure was amiably familiar to all such as enjoyed the Liberties of the Jug. For thirty years his mottled nose and the rubicundity of his cheeks were the ineffaceable ensigns of his intemperance. Yet there was a grimy humour in his forbidding aspect. The fusty black coat, which sat ill upon his shambling frame, was all besmirched with spilled snuff, and the lees of a thousand quart pots. The bands of his profession were ever awry upon a. tattered shirt. His ancient wig scattered dust and powder as he went, while a single buckle of some tawdry metal gave a look of oddity to his clumsy, slipshod feet. A caricature of a man, he ambled and chuckled and seized the easy pleasures within his reach. There was never a summer's day but he caught upon his brow the few faint gleams of sunlight that penetrated the gloomy yard. Hour after hour he would sit, his short fingers hardly linked across his belly, drinking his cup of ale, and puffing at a half-extinguished tobacco-pipe. Meanwhile he would reflect upon those triumphs of oratory which were his supreme delight. If it fell on a Monday that he took the air, a smile of satisfaction lit up his fat, loose features, for still he pondered the effect of yesterday's masterpiece. On Saturday the glad expectancy of tomorrow lent him a certain joyous dignity. At other times his eye lacked lustre, his gesture buoyancy, unless indeed he were called upon to follow the cart to Tyburn, or to compose the Last Dying Speech of some notorious malefactor.

Preaching was the master passion of his life. It was the pulpit that reconciled him to exile within a great city, and persuaded him to the enjoyment of roguish company. Those there were who deemed his career unfortunate; but a sense of fitness might have checked their pity, and it was only in his hours of maudlin confidence that the Reverend Thomas confessed to disappointment. Born of respectable parents in the County of Cambridgeshire, he nurtured his youth upon the exploits of James Hind and the Golden Farmer. His boyish pleasure was to lie in the ditch, which bounded his father's orchard, studying that now forgotten masterpiece, "There's no Jest like a True Jest." Then it was that he felt "immortal longings in his blood." He would take to the road, so he swore, and hold up his enemies like a gentleman. Once, indeed, he was surprised by the clergyman of the parish in act to escape from the rectory with two volumes of sermons and a silver flagon. The divine was minded to speak seriously to him concerning the dreadful sin of robbery, and having strengthened him with texts and good counsel, to send him forth unpunished. "Thieving and covetousness," said the parson, "must inevitably bring you to the gallows. If you would die in your bed, repent you of your evildoing, and rob no more." The exhortation was not lost upon Pureney, who, chastened in spirit, straightly prevailed upon his father to enter him a pensioner at Corpus Christi College in the University of Cambridge, that at the proper time he might take orders.

At Cambridge he gathered no more knowledge than was necessary for his profession, and wasted such hours as should have been given to study in drinking, dicing, and even less reputable pleasures. Yet repentance was always easy, and he accepted his first curacy, at Newmarket, with a brave heart and a good hopefulness. Fortunate was the choice of this early cure. Had he been gently guided at the outset, who knows but he might have lived out his life in respectable obscurity? But Newmarket then, as now, was a town of jollity and dissipation, and Pureney yielded without persuasion to the pleasures denied his cloth. There was ever a fire to extinguish at his throat, nor could he veil his wanton eye at the sight of a pretty wench. Again and again the lust of preaching urged him to repent, yet he slid back upon his past gaiety, until Parson. Pureney became a byword. Dismissed from Newmarket in disgrace, he wandered the country up and down in search of a pulpit, but so infamous became the habit of his life that only in prison could he find an audience fit and responsive.

And, in the nick, the chaplaincy of Newgate fell vacant. Here was the occasion to temper dissipation with piety, to indulge the twofold ambition of his life. What mattered it, if within the prison walls he dipped his nose more deeply into the punch-bowl than became a divine? The rascals would but respect him the more for his prowess, and knit more closely the bond of sympathy. Besides, after preaching and punch he best loved a penitent, and where in the world could he find so rich a crop of erring souls ripe for repentance as in gaol? Henceforth he might threaten, bluster, and cajole. If amiability proved fruitless he would put cruelty to the test, and terrify his victims by a spirited reference to Hell and to that Burning Lake they were so soon to traverse. At last, thought he, I shall be sure of my effect, and the prospect flattered his vanity. In truth, he won an immediate and assured success. Like the common file or cracksman, he fell into the habit of the place, intriguing with all the cleverness of a practised diplomatist, and setting one party against the other that he might in due season decide the trumpery dispute. The trusted friend of many a distinguished prig and murderer, he so intimately mastered the slang and etiquette of the Jug, that he was appointed arbiter of all those nice questions of honour which agitated the more reputable among the cross-coves. But these were the diversions of a strenuous mind, and it was in the pulpit or in the closet that the Reverend Thomas Pureney revealed his true talent.

As the ruffian had a sense of drama, so he was determined that his words should scald and bite the penitent. When the condemned pew was full of a Sunday his happiness was complete. Now his deep chest would hurl salvo on salvo of platitudes against the sounding-board; now his voice, lowered to a whisper, would coax the hopeless prisoners to prepare their souls. In a paroxysm of feigned anger he would crush the cushion with his clenched fist, or leaning over the pulpit side as though to approach the nearer to his victims, would roll a cold and bitter eye upon them, as of a cat watching caged birds. One famous gesture was irresistible, and he never employed it but some poor ruffian fell senseless to the floor. His stumpy fingers would fix a noose of air round some imagined neck, and so devoutly was the pantomime studied that you almost heard the creak of the retreating cart as the phantom culprit was turned off. But his conduct in the pulpit was due to no ferocity of temperament.

He merely exercised his legitimate craft. So long as Newgate supplied him with an enforced audience, so long would he thunder and bluster at the wrongdoer according to law and the dictates of his conscience.

Many, in truth, were his triumphs, but, as he would mutter in his garrulous old age, never was he so successful as in the last exhortation delivered to Matthias Brinsden. Now, Matthias Brinsden incontinently murdered his wife because she harboured too eager a love of the brandy-shop. A model husband, he had spared no pains in her correction. He had flogged her without mercy and without result. His one design was to make his wife obey him, which, as the Scriptures say, all wives should do. But the lust of gin overcame wifely obedience, and Brinsden, hoping for the best, was constrained to cut a hole in her skull. The next day she was as impudent as ever, until Matthias rose yet more fiercely in his wrath, and the shrew perished. Then was Thomas Pureney's opportunity, and the Sunday following the miscreant's condemnation he delivered unto him and seventeen other malefactors the moving discourse which here follows:

"We shall take our text," gruffed the Ordinary, "from out the Psalms: 'Bloodthirsty and deceitful men shall not live out half their days.' And firstly, we shall expound to you the heinous sin of murder, which is unlawful (1) according to the Natural Laws, (2) according to the Jewish Law, (3) according to the Christian Law, proportionably stronger. By Nature 'tis unlawful as 'tis injuring Society; as 'tis robbing God of what is His Right and Property; as 'tis depriving the Slain of the Satisfaction of Eating, Drinking, Talking, and the Light of the Sun, which it is his right to enjoy. And especially 'tis unlawful, as it is sending a Soul naked and unprepared to appear before a wrathful and avenging Deity without time to make his Soul composedly or to listen to the thoughtful ministrations of one (like ourselves) soundly versed in Divinity. By the Jewish Law 'tis forbidden, for is it not written (Gen. ix. 6): 'Whosoever sheddeth Man's Blood, by Man his Blood shall be shed'? And if an Eye be given for an Eye, a Tooth for a Tooth, how shall the Murderer escape with his dishonoured Life? 'Tis further forbidden by the Christian Law (proportionably stronger). But on this head we would speak no word, for were not you all, O miserable Sinners, born not in the Darkness of Heathendom, but in the burning Light of Christian England?

"Secondly, we will consider the peculiar wickedness of Parricide, and especially the Murder of a Wife. What deed, in truth, is more heinous than that a man should slay the Parent of his own Children, the Wife he had once loved and chose out of all the world to be a Companion of his Days; the Wife who long had shared his good Fortune and his ill, who had brought him with Pain and Anguish several Tokens and Badges of Affection, the Olive Branches round about his Table? To embrew the Hands in such blood is double Murder, as it murders not only the Person slain, but kills the Happiness of the orphaned Children, depriving them of Bread, and forcing them upon wicked Ways of getting a Maintenance, which often terminate in Newgate and an ignominious death.

"Bloodthirsty men, we have said, shall not live out half their Days. And think not that Repentance avails the Murderer. 'Hell and Damnation are never full' (Prov. xxvii. 20), and the meanest Sinner shall find a place in the Lake which burns unto Eternity with Fire and Brimstone. Alas! your Punishment shall not finish with the Noose. Your 'end is to be burned' (Heb. vi. 8), to be burned, for the Blood that is shed cries aloud for Vengeance." At these words, as Pureney would relate with a smile of recollected triumph, Matthias Brinsden screamed aloud, and a shiver ran through the idle audience which came to Newgate on a Black Sunday, as to a bull-baiting, Truly, the throng of thoughtless spectators hindered the proper solace of the Ordinary's ministrations, and many a respectable murderer complained of the intruding mob. But the Ordinary, otherwise minded, loved nothing so well as a packed house, and though he would invite the criminal to his private closet, and comfort his solitude with pious ejaculations, he would neither shield him from curiosity, nor tranquillise his path to the unquenchable fire.

Not only did he exercise in the pulpit a poignant and visible influence. He boasted the confidence of many heroes. His green old age cherished no more famous memory than the friendship of Jonathan Wild. He had known the Great Man at his zenith; he had wrestled with him in the hour of discomfiture; he had preached for his benefit that famous sermon on the text: "Hide Thy Face from my sins, and blot out all my Iniquities"; he had witnessed the hero's awful progress from Newgate to Tyburn; he had seen him shiver at the nubbing-cheat; he had composed for him a last dying speech, which did not shame the king of thief-takers, and whose sale brought a comfortable profit to the widow. Jonathan, on his side, had shown the Ordinary not a little condescension. It had been his whim, on the eve of his marriage, to present Mr. Pureney with a pair of white gloves, which were treasured as a priceless relic for many a year. And when he paid his last, forced visit to Newgate, he gave the Chaplain, for a pledge of his esteem, that famous silver staff, which he carried, as a badge of authority from the Government, the better to keep the people in awe, and favour the enterprises of his rogues.

Only one cloud shadowed this old and equal friendship. Jonathan had entertained the Ordinary with discourse so familiar, they had cracked so many a bottle together, that when the irrevocable sentence was passed, when he who had never shown mercy, expected none, the Great Man found the exhortations of the illiterate Chaplain insufficient for his high purpose. "As soon as I came into the condemned Hole," thus he wrote, "I began to think of making a preparation for my soul; and the better to bring my stubborn heart to repentance, I desired the advice of a man of learning, a man of sound judgment in divinity, and therefore application being made to the Reverend Mr. Nicholson, he very Christian-like gave me his assistance." Alas! Poor Pureney! He lacked subtlety, and he was instantly baffled, when the Great Man bade him expound the text: "Cursed is every one that hangeth on a tree." The shiftiest excuse would have brought solace to a breaking heart and conviction to a casuist brain. Yet for once the Ordinary was at a loss, and Wild, finding him insufficient for his purpose, turned a deaf ear to his ministrations. Thus he was rudely awakened from the dream of unnumbered sleepless nights. His large heart almost broke at the neglect.

But if his more private counsels were scorned, he still had the joy of delivering a masterpiece from the pulpit, of using "all the means imaginable to make Wild think of another world," and of seeing him as neatly turned off as the most exacting Ordinary could desire. And what inmate of Newgate ever forgot the afternoon of that glorious day (May the 24th, 1725)? Mr. Pureney returned to his flock, fortified with punch and good tidings. He pictured the scene at Tyburn with a bibulous circumstance, which admirably became his style, rejoicing, as he has rejoiced ever since, that, though he lost a friend, the honest rogue was saved at last from the machinations of the thief-taker.

So he basked and smoked and drank his ale, retelling the ancient stories, and hiccuping forth the ancient sermons. So, in the fading twilight of life, he smiled the smile of contentment, as became one who had emptied more quarts, had delivered more harrowing discourses, and had lived familiarly with more scoundrels than any devil-dodger of his generation.

SHEPPARD AND CARTOUCHE
I
JACK SHEPPARD

IT was midnight when Jack Sheppard reached the leads, wearied by his magical achievement, and still fearful of discovery. The "jolly pair of handcuffs," provided by the thoughtful Governor, lay discarded in his distant cell; the chains which a few hours since had grappled him to the floor encumbered the now useless staple. No trace of the ancient slavery disgraced him save the iron anklets which clung about his legs: though many a broken wall and shattered lock must serve for evidence of his prowess on the morrow. The Stone-jug was all be-chipped and shattered. From the castle he had forced his way through a nine-foot wall into the Red Room, whose bolts, bars, and hinges he had ruined to gain the Chapel. The road thence to the roof and to freedom was hindered by three stubborn iron doors; yet naught stood in the way of Sheppard's genius, and he was sensible, at last, of the night air chill upon his cheek.

But liberty was not yet: there was still a fall of forty feet, and he must needs repass the wreckage of his own making to filch the blankets from his cell. In terror lest he should awaken the Master-Side Debtors, he hastened back to the roof, lashed the coverlets together, and, as the city clocks clashed twelve, he dropped noiselessly upon the leads of a turner's house, built against the prison's outer wall. Behind him Newgate was cut out a black mass against the sky; at his feet glimmered the garret window of the turner's house, and behind the winking casement he could see the turner's servant going to bed. Through her chamber lay the road to glory and Clare Market, and breathlessly did Sheppard watch till the candle should be extinguished and the maid silenced in sleep. In his anxiety he must tarry—tarry; and for a weary hour he kicked his heels upon the leads, ambition still too uncertain for quietude. Yet he could not but catch a solace from his splendid craft. Said he to himself: "Am I not the most accomplished slip-string the world has known? The broken wall of every round house in town attests my bravery. Light-limbed though. I be, have I not forced the impregnable Castle itself? And my enemies—are they not to-day writhing in distress? The head of Blueskin, that pitiful thief, quivers in the noose; and Jonathan Wild bleeds at the throat from the dregs of a coward's courage. And what a triumph shall be mine when the Keeper finds the stronghold tenantless!

Now, unnumbered were the affronts he had suffered from the Keeper's impertinence, and he chuckled aloud at his own witty rejoinder. Only two days since the Gaoler had caught him tampering with his irons. "Young man," he had said, "I see what you have been doing, but the affair betwixt us stands thus: It is your business to make your escape, and mine to take care you shall not." Jack had answered coolly enough: "Then let's both mind our own business." And it was to some purpose that he had minded his. The letter to his baffled guardian, already sketched in his mind, tickled him afresh, when suddenly he leaps to his feet and begins to force the garret window.

The turner's maid was a heavy sleeper, and Sheppard crept from her garret to the twisted stair in peace, Once, on a lower floor, his heart beat faster at the trumpetings of the turner's nose, but he knew no check until he reached the street door. The bolt was withdrawn in an instant, but the lock was turned, and the key nowhere to be found. However, though the risk of disturbance was greater than in Newgate, the task was light enough: and with an iron link from his fetter, and a rusty nail which had served him bravely, the box was wrenched off in a trice, and Sheppard stood unattended in the Old Bailey. At first he was minded to make for his ancient haunts, or to conceal himself within the Liberty of Westminster; but the fetter-locks were still upon his legs, and he knew that detection would be easy as long as he was thus embarrassed. Wherefore, weary and an-hungered, he turned his steps northward, and never rested until he had gained Finchley Common.

At break of day, when the world re-awoke from the fear of thieves, he feigned a limp at a cottage door, and borrowed a hammer to straighten a pinching shoe. Five minutes behind a hedge, and his anklets had dropped from him; and, thus a free man, he took to the high road. After all he was persuaded to desert London and to escape a while from the sturdy embrace of Edgworth Bess. Moreover, if Bess herself were in the lock-up, he still feared the interested affection of Mistress Maggot, that other doxy, whose avarice would surely drive him upon a dangerous enterprise; so he struck across country, and kept starvation from him by petty theft. Up and down England he wandered in solitary insolence. Once, saith rumour, his lithe apparition startled the peace of Nottingham; once, he was well-nigh caught begging wort at a brew-house in Thames Street. But he might as well have lingered in Newgate as waste his opportunity so far from the delights of Town; the old lust of life still impelled him, and a week after the hue-and-cry was raised he crept at dead of night down Drury Lane. Here he found harbourage with a friendly fence, Wild's mortal enemy, who promised him a safe conduct across the seas. But the desire of work proved too strong for prudence; and in a fortnight he had planned an attack on the pawnshop of one Rawling, at the Four Balk in Drury Lane.

Now, Sheppard, whom no house ever built with hands was strong enough to hold, was better skilled at breaking out than at breaking in, and it is remarkable that his last feat in the cracking of cribs was also his greatest. Its very conception was a masterpiece of effrontery. Drury Lane was the thief-catcher's chosen territory; yet it was the Four Balls that Jack designed for attack, and watches, tie-wigs, snuff-boxes were among his booty. Whatever he could not crowd upon his person he presented to a brace of women. Tricked out in his stolen finery, he drank and swaggered in Clare Market. He was habited in a superb suit of black; a diamond fawney flashed upon his fam; his light tie-periwig was worth no less than seven pounds; pistols, tortoise-shell snuff-boxes, and golden guineas jostled one another in his pockets.

Thus, in brazen magnificence, he marched down Drury Lane on a certain Saturday night in November 1724. Towards midnight he visited Thomas Nicks, the butcher, and having bargained for three ribs of beef, carried Nicks with him to a chandler's hard by, that they might ratify the bargain with a dram. Unhappily, a boy from the "Rose and Crown" sounded the alarm; for coming into the chandler's for the empty ale-pots, he instantly recognised the incomparable gaol-thief, and lost no time in acquainting his master. Now, Mr. Bradford, of the "Rose and Crown," was a head-borough, who, with the zeal of a triumphant Dogberry, summoned the watch, and in less than half an hour Jack Sheppard was screaming blasphemies in a hackney-cab on his way home to Newgate.

The Stone-jug received him with deference and admiration. Three hundred pounds weight of irons were put upon him for an adornment, and the Governor professed so keen a solicitude for his welfare that he never left him unattended. There was scarce a beautiful woman in London who did not solace him with her condescension, and enrich him with her gifts. Not only did the President of the Royal Academy deign to paint his portrait, but (a far greater honour) Hogarth made him immortal. Even the King displayed a proper interest, demanding a full and precise account of his escapes. The hero himself was drunk with flattery; he bubbled with ribaldry; he touched off the most valiant of his contemporaries in a ludicrous phrase. But his chief delight was to illustrate his prowess to his distinguished visitors, and nothing pleased him better than to slip in and out of his chains.

Confronted with his judge, he forthwith proposed to rid himself of his handcuffs, and he preserved until the fatal tree an illimitable pride in his artistry. Nor would he believe in the possibility of death. To the very last he was confirmed in the hope of pardon; but, pardon failing him, his single consolation was that his procession from Westminster to Newgate was the largest that London had ever known, and that in the crowd a constable broke his leg. Even in the Condemned Hole he was unreconciled. If he had broken the Castle, why should he not also evade the gallows? Wherefore he resolved to carry a knife to Tyburn that he might cut the rope, and so, losing himself in the crowd, ensure escape. But the knife was discovered by his warder's vigilance, and taken from him after a desperate struggle. At the scaffold he behaved with admirable gravity: confessing the wickeder of his robberies, and asking pardon for his enormous crimes. "Of two virtues," he boasted at the self-same moment that the cart left him dancing without the music, "I have ever cherished an honest pride: never have I stooped to friendship with Jonathan Wild, or with any of his detestable thief-takers; and, though an undutiful son, I never damned my mother's eyes."

Thus died Jack Sheppard; intrepid burglar and incomparable artist, who, in his own separate ambition of prison-breaking, remains, and will ever remain, unrivalled. His most brilliant efforts were the result neither of strength nor of cunning; for so slight was he of build, so deficient in muscle, that both Edgworth Bess and Mistress Maggot were wont to bang him to their own mind and purpose. And an escape so magnificently planned, so bravely executed as was his from the Strong Room, is far greater than a mere effect of cunning. Those mysterious gifts which enable mankind to batter the stone walls of a prison, or to bend the iron bars of a cage, were pre-eminently his. It is also certain that he could not have employed his gifts in a more reputable profession

LOUIS-DOMINIQUE CARTOUCHE

OF all the heroes who have waged a private and undeclared war upon their neighbours, Louis-Dominique Cartouche was the most generously endowed. It was but his resolute contempt for politics, his unswerving love of plunder for its own sake, that prevented him from seizing a throne or questing after the empire of the world. The modesty of his ambition sets him below Caesar, or Napoleon, but he yields to neither in the genius of success: whatever he would attain was his on the instant, nor did failure interrupt his career, until treachery, of which he went in perpetual terror, involved himself and his comrades in ruin. His talent of general-ship was unrivalled. None of the gang was permitted the liberty of a free-lance. By Cartouche was the order given, and so long as the chief was in repose, Paris might enjoy her sleep. But when it pleased him to join battle a whistle was enough.

Now, it was revealed to his intelligence that the professional thief, who devoted all his days and such of his nights as were spared from depredation to wine and women, was more readily detected than the *valet-de-chambre,* who did but crack a crib or cry "Stand and deliver!" on a proper occasion. Wherefore, he bade his soldiers take service in the great houses of Paris, that, secure of suspicion, they might still be ready to obey the call of duty. Thus, also, they formed a reconnoitring force, whose vigilance no prize might elude; and nowhere did Cartouche display his genius to finer purpose than in this prudent disposition of his army. It remained only to efface himself, and therein he succeeded admirably by never sleeping two following nights in the same house: so that, when Cartouche was the terror of Paris, when even the King trembled in his bed, none knew his stature nor could recognise his features. In this shifting and impersonal vizard, he broke houses, picked pockets, robbed on the pad. One night he would terrify the Faubourg St. Germain; another he would plunder the humbler suburb of St. Antoine; but on each excursion he was companioned by experts, and the map of Paris was rigidly apportioned among his followers. To each district a captain was appointed, whose business it was to apprehend the customs of the quarter, and thus to indicate the proper season of attack.

Ever triumphant, with yellow-boys ever jingling in his pocket, Cartouche lived a life of luxurious merriment. A favourite haunt was a *cabaret* in the Rue Dauphine, chosen for the sanest of reasons, as his Captain Ferrand declared, that the landlady was a *femme d'esprit.* Here he would sit with his friends and his women, and thereafter drive his chariot across the Pont Neuf to the sunnier gaiety of the Palais-Royal. A finished dandy, he wore by preference a grey-white coat with silver buttons; his breeches and stockings were on a famous occasion of black silk; while a sword, scabbarded in satin, hung at his hip.

But if Cartouche, like many another great man, had the faculty of enjoyment, if he loved wine and wit, and mistresses handsomely attired in damask, he did not therefore neglect his art. When once the gang was perfectly ordered, murder followed robbery with so instant a frequency that Paris was panic-stricken. A cry of "Cartouche" straightway ensured an empty street. The King took counsel with his ministers: munificent rewards were offered, without effect. The thief was still at work in all security, and it was a pretty irony which urged him to strip and kill on the highway one of the King's own pages. Also, he did his work with so astonishing a silence, with so reasoned a certainty, that it seemed impossible to take him or his minions red-handed.

Before all, he discouraged the use of firearms. "A pistol," his philosophy urged, "is an excellent weapon in an emergency, but reserve it for emergencies. At close quarters it is none too sure; and why give the alarm against yourself?" Therefore he armed his band with loaded staves, which sent their enemies into a noiseless and fatal sleep. Thus was he wont to laugh at the police, deeming capture a plain impossibility. The traitor, in sooth, was his single, irremediable fear, and if ever suspicion was aroused against a member of the gang, that member was put to death with the shortest shrift.

Now, it happened in the last year of Cartouche's supremacy that a lily-livered comrade fell in love with a pretty dressmaker. The indiscretion was the less pardonable since the dressmaker had a horror of theft, and impudently tried to turn her lover from his trade. Cartouche, discovering the backslider, resolved upon a public exhibition. Before the assembled band he charged the miscreant with treason, and, cutting his throat, disfigured his face beyond recognition. Thereafter he pinned to the corse the following inscription, that others might be warned by so monstrous an example: "Ci gît Jean Rebâti, qui a eu le traitement qu'il méritait: ceux qui en feront autant que lui peuvent attendre le même sort." Yet this was the murder that led to the hero's own capture and death.

Du Châtelet, another craven, had already aroused the suspicions of his landlady: who, finding him something troubled the day after the traitor's death, and detecting a spot of blood on his neckerchief, questioned him closely. The coward fumbling at an answer, she was presently convinced of his guilt, and forthwith denounced him for a member of the gang to M. Pacôme, an officer of the Guard. Straightly did M. Pacôme summon Du Châtelet, and, assuming his guilt for certitude, bade him surrender his captain. "My friend," said he, "I know you for an associate of Cartouche. Your hands are soiled with murder and rapine. Confess the hiding-place of Cartouche, or in twenty-four hours you are broken on the wheel." Vainly did Du Châtelet protest his ignorance. M. Pacôme was resolute, and before the interview was over the robber confessed that Cartouche had given him rendezvous at nine next day.

In the grey morning thirty soldiers crept forth, "en habits de bourgeois et de chasseur," for the house where Cartouche had lain. It was an inn, kept by one Savard, near la Haulte Borne de la Courtille; and the soldiers, though they lacked not numbers, approached the chieftain's lair shaking with terror. In front marched Du Châtekt; the rest followed in Indian file, ten paces apart. When the traitor reached the house, Savard recognised him for a friend, and entertained him with familiar speech. "Is there anybody upstairs?" demanded Du Châtelet. "No," replied Savard. "Are the four women upstairs?" asked Du Châtelet again. "Yes, they are," came the answer: for Savard knew the password of the day. Instantly the soldiers filled the tavern, and, mounting the staircase, discovered Cartouche with his three lieutenants, Balagny, Limousin, and Blanchard. One of the four still lay abed; but Cartouche, with all the dandy's respect for his clothes, was mending his breeches. The others hugged a flagon of wine over the fire.

So fell the scourge of Paris into the grip of justice. But once under lock and key, he displayed all the qualities which made him supreme. His gaiety broke forth into a light-hearted contempt of his gaolers, and the Lieutenant Criminel, who would interrogate him, was covered with ridicule. Not for an instant did he bow to fate: all shackled as he was, his legs engarlanded in heavy chains—which he called his garters—he tempered his merriment with the meditation of escape. From the first he denied all knowledge of Cartouche, insisting that his name was Charles Bourguignon, and demanding burgundy, that he might drink to his country and thus prove him a true son of the soil. Not even the presence of his mother and brother abashed him. He laughed them away as impostors, hired by a false justice to accuse and to betray the innocent. No word of confession crossed his lips, and he would still entertain the officers of the law with joke and epigram.

Thus he won over a handful of the Guard, and, begging for solitude, he straightway set about escape with a courage and an address which Jack Sheppard might have envied. His delicate ear discovered that a cellar lay beneath his cell; and with the old nail which lies on the floor of every prison he made his way downwards into a boxmaker's shop. But a barking dog spoiled the enterprise: the boxmaker and his daughter were immediately abroad, and once more Cartouche was lodged in prison, weighted with still heavier garters.

Then came a period of splendid notoriety: he held his court, he gave an easy rein to his wit, he received duchesses and princes with an air of amiable patronage. Few there were of his visitants who left him without a present of gold, and thus the universal robber was further rewarded by his victims. His portrait hung in every house, and his thin, hard face, his dry, small features were at last familiar to the whole of France. M. Grandval made him the hero of an epic—"Le Vice Puni." Even the theatre was dominated by his presence; and while *Arlequin-Cartouche* was greeted with thunders of applause at the Italiens, the more serious Francais set *Cartouche* upon the stage in three acts, and lavished upon its theme the resources of a then intelligent art. M. Le Grand, author of the piece, deigned to call upon the king of thieves, spoke some words of *argot* with him, and by way of conscience money gave him a hundred crowns.

But Cartouche set little store by such patronage. He pocketed the crowns, and then put an end to the comedy by threatening that if it were played again the companions of Cartouche would punish all such miscreants as dared to make him a laughing-stock. For Cartouche would endure ridicule at no man's hand. At the very instant of his arrest, all barefooted as he was, he kicked a constable who presumed to smile at his discomfiture. His last days were spent in resolute abandonment. True, he once attempted to beat out his brains with the fetters that bound him; true also, he took a poison that had been secretly conveyed within the prison. But both attempts failed, and, more scrupulously watched, he had no other course than jollity. Lawyers and priests he visited with a like and bitter scorn, and when, on November 27, 1721, he was led to the scaffold, not a word of confession or contrition had been dragged from him.

To the last moment he cherished the hope of rescue, and eagerly he scanned the crowd for the faces of his comrades. But the gang, trusting to its leader's nobility, had broken its oath. With contemptuous dignity Cartouche determined upon revenge: proudly he turned to the priest, begging a respite and the opportunity of speech. Forgotten by his friends, he resolved to spare no single soul: he betrayed even his mistresses to justice. Of his gang, forty were in the service of Mlle, de Montpensier, who was already in Spain; while two obeyed the Duchesse de Ventadour as *valets-de-pied.* His confession, in brief, was so dangerous a document, it betrayed the friends and servants of so many great houses, that the officers of the Law found safety for their patrons in its destruction, and not a line of the hero's testimony remains. The trial of his comrades dragged on for many a year, and after Cartouche had been cruelly broken on the wheel, not a few of the gang, of which he had been at once the terror and the inspiration, suffered a like fate. Such the career and such the fitting end of the most distinguished marauder the world has known. Thackeray, with no better guide than a chap-book, was minded to belittle him, now habiting him like a scullion, now sending him forth on some petty errand of cly-faking. But for all Thackeray's contempt his fame is still un-dimmed, and he has left the reputation of one who, as thief unrivalled, had scarce his equal as wit and dandy even in the days when Louis the Magnificent was still a memory and an example.

III
A PARALLEL

(SHEPPARD AND CARTOUCHE)

IF the seventeenth century was the golden age of the hightobyman, it was at the advent of the eighteenth that the burglar and street-robber plied their trade with the most distinguished success, and it was the good fortune of both Cartouche and Sheppard to be born in the nick of time. Rivals in talent, they were also near contemporaries, and the Scourge of Paris may well have been famous in the purlieus of Clare Market before Jack the Slip-String paid the last penalty of his crimes. As each of these great men harboured a similar ambition, so their careers are closely parallel. Born in a humble rank of life, Jack, like Cartouche, was the architect of his own fortune; Jack, like Cartouche, lived to be flattered by noble dames and to claim the solicitude of his Sovereign; and each owed his pre-eminence rather to natural genius than to a sympathetic training.

But, for all the Briton's artistry, the Frenchman was in all points save one the superior. Sheppard's brain carried him not beyond the wants of to-day and the extortions of Poll Maggot. Who knows but he might have been a respectable citizen, with never a chance for the display of his peculiar talent, had not hunger and his mistress's greed driven him upon the pad? History records no brilliant robbery of his own planning, and so circumscribed was his imagination that he must needs pick out his own friends and benefactors for depredation. His paltry sense of discipline permitted him to be betrayed even by his brother and pupil, and there was no cracksman of his time over whose head he held the rod of terror. Even his hatred of Jonathan Wild was the result not of policy but of prejudice. Cartouche, on the other hand, was always perfect when at work. The master of himself, he was also the master of his fellows. There was no detail of civil war that he had not made his own, and he still remains, after nearly two centuries, the greatest captain the world has seen. Never did he permit an enterprise to fail by accident; never was he impelled by hunger or improvidence to fight a battle unprepared. His means were always neatly fitted to their end, as is proved by the truth that, throughout his career, he was arrested but once, and then not by his own inadvertence but by the treachery of others.

Yet from the moment of arrest Jack Sheppard asserted his magnificent superiority. If Cartouche was a sorry bungler at prison-breaking, Sheppard was unmatched in this dangerous art. The sport of the one was to break in, of the other to break out. True, the Briton proved his inferiority by too frequently placing himself under lock and key; but you will forgive his every weakness for the unexampled skill wherewith he extricated himself from the stubbornest dungeon. Cartouche would scarce have given Sheppard a menial's office in his gang. How cordially Sheppard would have despised Cartouche's solitary experiment in escape! To be foiled by a dog and a boxmaker's daughter! Would not that have seemed contemptible to the master breaker of those unnumbered doors and walls which separate the Castle from the freedom of Newgate roof?

Such, then, is the contrast between the heroes. Sheppard claims our admiration for one masterpiece. Cartouche has a sheaf of works, which shall carry him triumphantly to the remotest future. And when you forget a while professional rivalry, and consider the delicacies of leisure, you will find the Frenchman's greatness still indisputable. At all points he was the prettier gentleman. Sheppard, to be sure, had a sense of finery, but he was so unused to grandeur, that vulgarity always spoiled his effects. When he hied him from the pawnshop, laden with booty, he must e'en cram what he could not wear into his pockets; and doubtless his vulgar lack of reticence made detection easier. Cartouche, on the other hand, had an unfailing sense of proportion, and was never more dressed than became the perfect dandy. He was elegant, he was polished, he was joyous. He drank wine, while the other soaked himself in beer; he despised whatever was common, while his rival knew but the coarser flavours of life.

The one was distinguished by a boisterous humour, a swaggering pride in his own prowess; the wit of the other might be edged like a knife, nor would he ever appeal for a spectacle to the curiosity of the mob. Both were men of many mistresses, but again in his conduct with women Cartouche showed an honester talent. Sheppard was at once the prey and the whipping-block of his two infamous doxies, who agreed in deformity of feature as in contempt for their lover. Cartouche, on the other hand, chose his *cabaret* for the wit of its *patronney* and was always happy in the elegance and accomplishment of his companions. One point of likeness remains. The two heroes resembled each other not only in their profession, but in their person. Though their trade demanded physical strength, each was small and slender of build. "A little slight-limbed lad," says the historian of Sheppard. "A thin, spare frame," sings the poet of Cartouche. Here, then, neither had the advantage, and if in the shades Cartouche despises the clumsiness and vulgarity of his rival, Sheppard may still remember the glory of Newgate, and twit the Frenchman with the barking of the boxmaker's dog. But genius is the talent of the dead, and the wise, who are not partisans, will not deny to the one or to the other the possession of the rarer gift.

VAUX

TO Haggart, who babbled on the Castle Rock of Wullie Wallace and was only nineteen when he danced without the music; to Simms, *alias* Gentleman Harry, who showed at Tyburn how a hero could die; to George Barrington, the incomparably witty and adroit—to these a full meed of honour has been paid. Even the coarse and dastardly Freney has achieved, with Thackeray's aid (and Lever's) something of a reputation. But James Hardy Vaux, despite his eloquent bid for fame, has not found his rhapsodist. Yet a more consistent ruffian never pleaded for mercy. From his early youth until in 1819 he sent forth his *Memoirs* to the world, he lived industriously upon the cross. There was no racket but he worked it with energy and address. Though he practised the more glorious crafts of pickpocket and shoplifter, he did not despise the begging-letter, and he suffered his last punishment for receiving what another's courage had conveyed. His enterprise was not seldom rewarded with success, and for a decade of years he continued to preserve an appearance of gentility; but it is plain, even from his own narrative, that he was scarce an artist, and we shall best understand him if we recognise that he was a Philistine among thieves. He lived in an age of pocket-picking, and skill in this branch is the true test of his time. A contemporary of Barrington, he had before him the most brilliant of examples, which might properly have enforced the worth of a simple method. But, though he constantly brags of his success at Drury Lane, we take not his generalities for gospel, and the one exploit whose credibility is enforced with circumstance was pitiful both in conception and performance. A meeting of freeholders at the "Mermaid Tavern," Hackney, was the occasion, and after drawing blank upon blank, Vaux succeeded at last in extracting a silver snuff-box. Now, his clumsiness had suggested the use of the scissors, and the victim not only discovered the scission in his coat, but caught the thief with the implements of his art upon him. By a miracle of impudence Vaux escaped conviction, but he deserved the gallows for his want of principle, and not even sympathy could have let drop a tear, had justice seized her due. On the straight or on the cross the canons of art deserve respect; and a thief is great, not because he is a thief, but because, in filling his own pocket, he preserves from violence the legitimate traditions of his craft.

But it was in conflict with the jewellers that Vaux best proved his mettle. It was his wont to clothe himself "in the most elegant attire," and on the pretence of purchase to rifle the shops of Piccadilly. For this offence—"pinching" the Cant Dictionary calls it—he did his longest stretch of time, and here his admirable qualities of cunning and coolness found their most generous scope. A love of fine clothes he shared with all the best of his kind, and he visited Mr. Bilger—the jeweller who arrested him—magnificently arrayed. He wore a black coat and waistcoat, blue pantaloons, Hessian boots, and a hat "in the extreme of the newest fashion." He was also resplendent with gold watch and eye-glass. His hair was powdered, and a fawney sparkled on his dexter fam. The booty was enormous, and a week later he revisited the shop on another errand. This second visit was the one flash of genius in a somewhat drab career: the jeweller was so completely dumfounded, that Vaux might have got clean away. But though he kept discreetly out of sight for a while, at last he drifted back to his ancient boozing-ken, and was there betrayed to a notorious thief-catcher. The inevitable sentence of death followed. It was commuted after the fashion of the time, and Vaux, having sojourned a while at the Hulks, sought for a second time the genial airs of Botany Bay.

His vanity and his laziness were alike invincible. He believed himself a miracle of learning as well as a perfect thief, and physical toil was the sole "lay" for which he professed no capacity. For a while he corrected the press for a printer, and he roundly asserts that his knowledge of literature and of foreign tongues rendered him invaluable. It was vanity again that induced him to assert his innocence when he was lagged for so vulgar a crime as stealing a wipe from a tradesman in Chancery Lane. At the moment of arrest he was on his way to purchase base coin from a White-chapel bit-faker: but, despite his nefarious errand, he is righteously wrathful at what he asserts was an unjust conviction, and henceforth he assumed the crown of martyrdom. His first and last ambition during the intervals of freedom was gentility, and so long as he was not at work he lived the life of a respectable grocer. Although the casual Cyprian flits across his page, he pursued the one flame of his life for the good motive, and he affects to be a very model of domesticity. The sentiment of piety also was strong upon him, and if he did not, like the illustrious Peace, pray for his jailer, he rivalled the Prison Ordinary in comforting the condemned. Had it only been his fate to die on the gallows, how unctuous had been his croak!

The text of his "Memoirs" having been edited, it is scarce possible to define his literary talent. The book, as it stands, is an excellent piece of narrative, but it loses somewhat by the pretence of style. The man's invulnerable conceit prevented an absolute frankness, and there is little enough hilarity to correct the acid sentiment and the intolerable vows of repentance. Again, though he knows his subject, and can patter flash with the best, his incorrigible respectability leads him to ape the manner of a Grub Street hack, and to banish to a vocabulary those pearls of slang which might have added vigour and lustre to his somewhat tiresome page. However, the thief cannot escape his inevitable defects. The vanity, the weakness, the sentimentality of those who are born beasts of prey, yet have the faculty of depredation only half-developed, are the foes of truth, and it is well to remember that the autobiography of a rascal is tainted at its source. A congenital pickpocket, equipped with the self-knowledge and the candour which would enable him to recognise himself an outlaw and justice his enemy rather than an instrument of malice, would prove a Napoleon rather than a Vaux. So that we must e'en accept our Newgate Calendar with its many faults upon its head, and be content. For it takes a man of genius to write a book, and the thief who turns author commonly inhabits a paradise of the second-rate.

GEORGE BARRINGTON

AS Captain Hind was master of the road, George Barrington was (and remains for ever) the absolute monarch of pickpockets. Though the art, superseding the cutting of purses, had been practised with courage and address for half a century before Barrington saw the light, it was his own incomparable genius that raised thievery from the dangerous valley of experiment, and set it, secure and honoured, upon the mountain height of perfection. To a natural habit of depredation, which, being a man of letters, he was wont to justify, he added a sureness of hand, a fertility of resource, a recklessness of courage which drove his contemporaries to an amazed respect, and from which none but the Philistine will withhold his admiration. An accident discovered his taste and talent. At school he attempted to kill a companion—the one act of violence which sullies a strangely gentle career; and outraged at the affront of a flogging, he fled with twelve guineas and a gold repeater watch. A vulgar theft this, and no presage of future greatness; yet it proves the fearless greed, the contempt of private property, which mark as with a stigma the temperament of the prig. His faculty did not rust long for lack of use, and at Drogheda, when he was but sixteen, he encountered one Price, half barn-stormer, half thief. Forthwith he embraced the twin professions, and in the interlude of more serious pursuits is reported to have made a respectable appearance as Jaffier in **Venice Preserved.** For a while he dreamed of Drury Lane and glory; but an attachment for Miss Egerton, the Belvidera to his own Jaffier, was more costly than the barns of Londonderry warranted, and, with Price for a colleague, he set forth on a tour of robbery, merely interrupted through twenty years by a few periods of enforced leisure.

His youth, indeed, was his golden age. For four years he practised his art, chilled by no shadow of suspicion, and his immunity was due as well to his excellent bearing as to his sleight of hand. In one of the countless chap-books which dishonour his feme, he is unjustly accused of relying for his effects upon an elaborate apparatus, half knife, half scissors, wherewith to rip the pockets of his victims. The mere back-biting of envy! An artistic triumph was never won save by legitimate means; and the hero who plundered the Duke of L—r at Ranelagh, who emptied the pockets of his acquaintance without fear of exposure, who all but carried off the priceless snuff-box of Count Orloff, most assuredly followed his craft in full simplicity and with a proper scorn of clumsy artifice. At his first appearance he was the master, sumptuously apparelled, with Price for valet. At Dublin his birth and quality were never questioned, and when he made a descent upon London it was in company with Captain W. H—n, who remained for years his loyal friend. He visited Brighton ad the chosen companion of Lord Ferrers and the wicked Lord Lyttelton. His manners and learning were alike irresistible. Though the picking of pockets was the art and interest of his life, he was on terms of easy familiarity with light literature, and he considered no toil too wearisome if only his conversation might dazzle his victims. Two maxims he charactered upon his heart: the one, never to run a large risk for a small gain; the other, never to forget the carriage and diction of a gentleman.

He never stooped to pilfer, until exposure and decay had weakened his hand. In his first week at Dublin he carried off £1000, and it was only his fateful interview with Sir John Fielding that gave him poverty for a bedfellow. Even at the end, when he slunk from town to town, a notorious outlaw, he had inspirations of his ancient magnificence, and —at Chester—he eluded the vigilance of his enemies and captured £600, wherewith he purchased some months of respectability. Now, respectability was ever dear to him, and it was at once his pleasure and profit to live in the highest society. Were it not blasphemy to sully Barrington with slang you would call him a member of the swell-mob, but, having cultivated a grave and sober style for himself, he recoiled in horror from the flash lingo, and his susceptibility demands respect.

He kept a commonplace book! Was ever such thrift in a thief? Whatever images or thoughts flashed through his brain, he seized them on paper, even "amidst the jollity of a tavern, or in the warmth of an interesting conversation." Was it then strange that he triumphed as a man of fashionable and cultured leisure? He would visit Ranelagh with the most distinguished, and turn a while from epigram and jest to empty the pocket of a rich acquaintance. And ever with so tactful a certainty, with so fine a restraint of the emotions, that suspicion was preposterous. To catalogue his exploits is superfluous, yet let it be recorded that once he went to Court, habited as a clergyman, and came home the richer for a diamond order, Lord C—'s

proudest decoration. Even the assault upon Prince Orloff was nobly planned. Barrington had precise intelligence of the marvellous snuff-box—the Empress's own
gift to her lover; he knew also how he might meet the Prince at Drury Lane; he had
even discovered that the Prince for safety hid the jewel in his vest. But the Prince
felt the Prig's hand upon the treasure, and gave an instant alarm. Over-confidence,
maybe, or a too liberal dinner was the cause of failure, and Barrington, surrounded
in a moment, was speedily in the lock-up. It was the first rebuff that the hero had
received, and straightway his tact and ingenuity left him. The evidence was faulty,
the prosecution declined, and naught was necessary for escape save presence of
mind. Even friends were staunch, and had Barrington told his customary lie, his
character had gone unsullied. Yet having posed for his friends as a student of the
law, at Bow Street he must needs declare himself a doctor, and the needless discrep-
ancy ruined him. Though he escaped the gallows, there was an end to the diversions
of intellect and fashion; as he discovered when he visited the House of Lords to hear
an appeal, and Black Rod ejected him at the persuasion of Mr. G—. As yet unused
to insult, he threatened violence against the aggressor, and finding no bail he was
sent on his first imprisonment to the Bridewell in Tothill Fields. Rapid, indeed, was
the descent. At the first grip of adversity, he forgot his cherished principles, and two
years later the loftiest and most elegant gentleman that ever picked a pocket was
at the Hulks—for robbing a harlot at Drury Lane! Henceforth, his insolence and
artistry declined, and, though to the last there were intervals of grandeur, he spent
the better part of fifteen years in the commission of crimes, whose very littleness
condemned them. At last an exile from St. James's and Ranelagh, he was forced into
a society which still further degraded him. Hitherto he had shunned the society of
professed thieves; in his golden youth he had scorned to shelter him in the flash
kens, which were the natural harbours of pickpockets. But now, says his biographer, he began to seek evil company, and, the victim of his own fame, found safety
only in obscene concealment.

At the Hulks he recovered something of his dignity, and discretion rendered his
first visit brief enough. Even when he was committed on a second offence, and had
attempted suicide, he was still irresistible, and he was discharged with several years
of imprisonment to run. But, in truth, he was born for honour and distinction, and
common actions, common criminals, were in the end distasteful to him. In his hey-

day he stooped no further than to employ such fences as might profitably dispose of his booty, and the two partners of his misdeeds were both remarkable. James, the earlier accomplice, affected clerical attire, and in 1791 "was living in a Westphalian monastery, to which he some years ago retired, in an enviable state of peace and penitence, respected for his talents, and loved for his amiable manners, by which he is distinguished in an eminent degree." The other ruffian, Lowe by name, was known to his own Bloomsbury Square for a philanthropic and cultured gentleman, yet only suicide saved him from the gallows. And while Barrington was wise in the choice of his servants, his manners drove even strangers to admiration. Policemen and prisoners were alike anxious to do him honour. Once when he needed money for his own defence, his brother thieves, whom he had ever shunned and despised, collected £100 for the captain of their guild. Nor did gaoler and judge ever forget the respect due to a gentleman. When Barrington was tried and condemned for the theft of Mr. Townsend's watch at Enfield Races—September 15, 1790, was the day of his last transgression—one knows not which was the more eloquent in his respect, the judge or the culprit.

But it was not until the pickpocket set out for Botany Bay that he took full advantage of his gentle manly bearing. To thrust "Mr." Barrington into the hold was plainly impossible, even though transportation for seven years was his punishment. Wherefore he was admitted to the boatswain's mess, was allowed as much baggage as a first-class passenger, and doubtless beguiled the voyage (for others) with the information of a well-stored mind. By an inspiration of luck he checked a mutiny, holding the quarter-deck against a mob of ruffians with no weapon but a marline-spike. And hereafter, as he tells you in his "Voyage to New South Wales," he was accorded the fullest liberty to come or go. He visited many a foreign port with the officers of the ship; he packed a hundred note-books with trite and superfluous observations; he posed, in brief, as the captain of the ship without responsibility. Arrived at Port Jackson, he was acclaimed a hero, and received with obsequious solicitude by the Governor, who promised that his "future situation should be such as would render his banishment from England as little irksome as possible." Forthwith he was appointed high constable of Paramatta, and, like Vautrin, who might have taken the youthful Barrington for another Rastignac, he ended his days the honourable custodian of less fortunate convicts. Or, as a broadside ballad has it,

He left old Drury's flash purlieus, To turn at last a copper.

Never did he revert to his ancient practice. If in his youth he had lived the double-life with an effrontery and elegance which Brodie himself never attained, henceforth his career was single in its innocence. He became a prig in the less harmful and more offensive sense. After the orthodox fashion he endeared himself to all who knew him, and ruled Paramatta with an equable severity. Having cultivated the humanities for the base purposes of his trade, he now devoted himself to literature with an energy of dulness, becoming, as it were, a liberal education personified. His earlier efforts had been in verse, and you wonder that no enterprising publisher had ventured on a limited edition, Time was he composed an ode to Light, and once recovering from a fever contracted at Ballyshannon, he addressed a few burning lines to Hygeia:

Hygeia! thou whose eyes display The lustre of meridian day;

and so on for endless couplets. Then, had he not celebrated in immortal verse his love for Miss Egerton, untimely drowned in the waters of the Boyne? But now, as became the Constable of Paramatta, he chose the sterner medium, and followed up his "Voyage to New South Wales" with several exceeding trite and valuable histories.

His most ambitious work was dedicated in periods of unctuous piety to his Majesty King George III., and the book's first sentence is characteristic of his method and sensibility: "In contemplating the origin, rise, and fall of nations, the mind is alternately filled with a mixture of sacred pain and pleasure." Would you read further? Then you will find Fauna and Flora, twin goddesses of ineptitude, flitting across the page, unreadable as a geographical treatise. His first masterpiece was translated into French, *anno* VI., and the translator apologises that war with England alone prevents the compilation of a suitable biography. Was ever thief treated with so grave a consideration? Then, another work was prefaced by the Right Hon. William Eden, and all were "embellished with beautiful coloured plates," and ran through several editions. Once only did he return to poetry, the favoured medium of his youth, and he returned to write an imperishable line. But even then his priggishness persuaded him to renounce the authorship, and to disparage the achievement. The occasion was the opening of a theatre at Sydney, wherein the parts were sustained by convicts. The cost of admission to the gallery was one shilling, paid in money, flour, meat, or spirits. The play was entitled *The Revenge and the Hotel,* and Barrington provided the prologue, which for one passage is for ever memorable. Thus it runs:

From distant climes, o'er widespread seas, we come, Though not with much eclat or beat of drum; True patriots we, for be it understood, We left our country for our country's good. No private views disgraced our generous zeal, What urged our travels was our country's weal; And none will doubt, but that our emigration Has proved most useful to the British nation.

"We left our country for our country's good." That line, thrown fortuitously into four hundred pages of solid prose, has emerged to become the common possession of Fleet Street. It is the man's one title to literary fame, for spurning the thievish practice he knew so well, be was righteously indignant when *The London Spy* was fathered upon him. Though he emptied his contemporary's pockets of many thousands, he enriched the Dictionary of Quotations with one line, which will be repeated so long as there is human hand to wield a pen. And, if the High Constable of Paramatta was tediously respectable, George Barrington, the Prig, was a man of genius.

THE SWITCHER AND GENTLEMAN HARRY
I
THE SWITCHER

DAVID HAGGART was born at Canonmills, with no richer birthright than thievish fingers and a left hand of surpassing activity. The son of a gamekeeper, he grew up a long-legged, red-headed callant, lurking in the sombre shadow of the Cowgate, or like the young Sir Walter, championing the Auld Town against the New on the slopes of Arthur's Seat, Kipping was his early sin; but the sportsman's instinct, born of his father's trade, was so strong within him, that he pinched a fighting cock before he was breeched, and risked the noose for horse stealing when marbles should have engrossed his boyish fancy. Turbulent and lawless, he bitterly resented the intolerable restraint of a tranquil life, and, at last, in the hope of a larger liberty, he enlisted for a drummer in the Norfolk Militia, stationed at the moment in Edinburgh Castle. A brief, insubordinate year, misspent in his country's service, proved him hopeless of discipline: he claimed his discharge, and henceforth he was free to follow the one craft for which nature and his own ambition had moulded him.

Like Chatterton, like Rimbaud, Haggart came into the full possession of his talent while still a child. A Barrington of fourteen, he knew every turn and twist of his craft, before he escaped from school. His youthful necessities were munificently supplied by facile depredation, and the only hindrance to immediate riches was his ignorance of the flash kens where he might fence his plunder. Meanwhile he painted his soul black with wickedness. Such hours as he could snatch from the profitable conduct of his trade he devoted to the austere debauchery of Leith or the Golden Acre. Though he knew not the seduction of whisky, he missed never a dance nor a raffle, joining the frolics of prigs and callets in complete forgetfulness of the shorter catechism. In vain the kirk compared him to a "bottle in the smoke"; in vain the minister whispered of hell and the gallows; his heart hardened, as his fingers grew agile, and when, at sixteen, he left his father's house for a sporting life, he had not his equal in the three kingdoms for cunning and courage.

His first accomplice was Barney McGuire, who— until a fourteen stretch sent him to Botany Bay—played Clytus to David's Alexander, and it was at Portobello races that their brilliant partnership began. Hitherto Haggart had worked by stealth; he had tracked his booty under the cloud of night. Now was the moment to prove his prowess in the eye of day, to break with a past which he already deemed ignoble. His heart leapt with the occasion: he tackled his adventure with the hothead energy of a new member, big with his maiden speech. The victim was chosen in an instant: a backer, whose good fortune had broken the bookmakers. There was no thief on the course who did not wait, in hungry appetence, the sportsman's descent from the stand; yet the novice outstripped them all. "I got the first dive at his keek-cloy," he writes in his simple, heroic style, "and was so eager on my prey, that I pulled out the pocket along with the money, and nearly upset the gentleman." A steady brain saved him from the consequence of an o'erbuoyant enthusiasm. The notes were passed to Barney in a flash, and when the sportsman turned upon his assailant, Haggart's hands were empty.

Thereupon followed an infinite series of brilliant exploits. With Barney to aid, he plundered the Border like a reiver. He stripped the yeomen of Tweedside with a ferocity which should have avenged the disgrace of Flodden. More than once he ransacked Ecclefechan, though it is unlikely that he emptied the lean pocket of Thomas Carlyle. There was not a gaff from Newcastle to the Tay which he did not haunt with sedulous perseverance; nor was he confronted with failure, until his figure became a universal terror. His common method was to price a horse, and while the dealer showed Barney the animal's teeth, Haggart would slip under the uplifted arm, and ease the blockhead of his blunt. Arrogant in his skill, delighted with his manifold triumphs, Haggart led a life of unbroken prosperity under the brisk air of heaven, and, despite the risk of his profession, he remained two years a stranger to poverty and imprisonment. His worse mishap was to slip his forks into an empty pocket, or to encounter in his cups a milvadering horse-dealer; but his joys were free and frank, while he exulted in his success with a boyish glee. "I was never happier in all my life than when I fingered all this money," he exclaims when he had captured the comfortable prize of two hundred pounds. And then he would make merry at Newcastle or York, forgetting the knowing ones for a while, going abroad in white cape and tops, and flicking his leg like a gentleman with a dandy whip. But at last Barney and a wayward ambition persuaded him to desert his proper craft for the greater hazard of cracking a crib, and thus he was involved in his ultimate ruin. He incurred and he deserved the untoward fate of those who overlook their talents' limitation; and when this master of pickpockets followed Barney through the window of a secluded house upon the York Road, he might already have felt the noose tightening at his neck. The immediate reward of this bungled attack was thirty pounds, but two days later he was committed with Barney to the Durham Assizes, where he exchanged the obscurity of the perfect craftsman for the notoriety of the dangerous gaol-bird.

For the moment, however, he recovered his freedom: breaking prison, he straightway conveyed a fiddlestick to his comrade, and in a twinkling was at Newcastle again, picking up purses well lined with gold, and robbing the bumpkins of their scouts and chats. But the time of security was overpast. Marked and suspicious, he began to fear the solitude of the country; he left the horse-fair for the city, and sought in the budging-kens of Edinburgh the secrecy impossible on the hill-side. A clumsy experiment in shoplifting doubled his danger, and more than once he saw the inside of the police-office. Henceforth, he was free of the family; he loafed in the Shirra-Brae; he knew the flash houses of Leith and the Grassmarket. With Jean Johnston, the blowen of his choice, he smeared his hands with the squalor of petty theft, and the drunken recklessness wherewith he swaggered it abroad hastened his approaching downfall.

With a perpetual anxiety to avoid the nippers his artistry dwindled. The left hand, invincible on the Cheviots, seemed no better than a bunch of thumbs in the narrow ways of Edinburgh; and after innumerable misadventures Haggart was safely lodged in Dumfries gaol. No sooner was he locked within his cell than his restless brain planned a generous escape. He would win liberty for his fellows as well as for himself, and after a brief council a murderous plot was framed and executed. A stone slung in a handkerchief sent the gaoler to sleep; the keys found on him opened the massy doors; and Haggart was free with a reward set upon his head. The shock of the enterprise restored his magnanimity. Never did he display a finer bravery than in this spirited race for his life, and though three counties were aroused he doubled and ducked to such purpose that he outstripped John Richardson himself with all his bloodhounds, and two days later marched into Carlisle disguised in the stolen rags of a potato-bogle.

During the few months that remained to him of life he embarked upon a veritable Odyssey: he scoured Scotland from the Border to St. Andrews, and finally contrived a journey oversea to Ireland, where he made the name of Daniel O'Brien a terror to well-doers. Insolent and careless, he lurched from prison to prison; now it was Armagh that held him, now Down-patrick, until at last he was thrust on a general charge of vagabondage and ill-company into Kilmainham, which has since harboured many a less valiant adventurer than David Haggart. Here the culminating disgrace overtook him: he was detected in the prison yard by his ancient enemy, John Richardson, of Dumfries, who dragged him back to Scotland heavily shackled and charged with murder. So nimble had he proved himself in extrication, that his captors secured him with pitiless severity; round his waist he carried an iron belt, whereto were padlocked the chains, clanking at his wrists and ankles. Thus tortured and helpless, he was fed "like a sucking turkey in Bedlam"; but his sorrows vanished, and his dying courage revived at sight of the torchlight procession, which set forth from Dumfries to greet his return.

His coach was hustled by a mob, thousands strong, eager to catch sight of Haggart the Murderer, and though the spot where he slew Morrin was like fire beneath his passing feet, he carried to his cell a heart and a brain aflame with gratified vanity. His guilt being patent, reprieve was as hopeless as acquittal, and after the assured condemnation he spent his last few days with what profit he might in religious and literary exercises. He composed a memoir, which is a model of its kind; so diligently did he make his soul, that he could appear on the scaffold in a chastened spirit of prayerful gratitude; and, being an eminent scoundrel, he seemed a proper subject for the ministrations of Mr. George Combe. "That is the one thing I did not know before," he confessed with an engaging modesty, when his bumps were squeezed, and yet he was more than a match for the amiable phrenologist, whose ignorance of mankind persuaded him to believe that an illiterate felon could know himself and analyse his character.

But his character escaped his critics as it escaped himself. Time was when George Borrow, that other picaroon, surprised the youthful David, thinking of Willie Wallace upon the Castle Rock, and Lavengro's romantic memory transformed the raw-boned pickpocket into a monumental hero, who lacked nothing save a vast theatre to produce a vast effect. He was a Tamerlane, robbed of his opportunity; a valiant warrior, who looked in vain for a battlefield; a marauder who climbed the scaffold not for the magnitude, but for the littleness of his sins. Thus Borrow, in complete misunderstanding of the rascal's qualities.

Now, Haggart's ambition was as circumscribed as his ability. He died, as he was born, an expert cly-faker, whose achievements in sleight of hand are as yet unparalleled. Had the world been one vast breast-pocket his fish-hook fingers would have turned it inside out, But it was not his to mount a throne, or overthrow a dynasty. "My forks," he boasted, "are equally long, and they never fail me." That is at once the reason and the justification of hid triumph. Born with a consummate artistry tingling at his finger-tips, how should he escape the compulsion of a glorious destiny? Without fumbling or failure he discovered the single craft for which fortune had framed him, and he pursued it with; a courage and an industry which gave him not a kingdom, but fame and booty, exceeding even his greedy aspiration. No Tamerlane he, questing for a continent, but David Haggart, the man with the long forks, happy if he snatched his neighbour's purse.

Before all things he respected the profession which his left hand made inevitable, and which he pursued with unconquerable pride. Nor in his inspired youth was plunder his sole ambition: he cultivated the garden of his style with the natural zeal of the artist; he frowned upon the bungler with a lofty contempt. His materials were simplicity itself; his forks, which were always with him, and another's well-filled pocket, since, sensible of danger, he cared not to risk his neck for a purse that did not contain so much as would "sweeten a grawler." At its best, his method was always witty—that is the single word which will characterise it—witty as a piece of Heine's prose, and as dangerous. He would run over a man's pockets while he spoke with him, returning what he chose to discard without the lightest breath of suspicion. "A good workman," his contemporaries called him; and they thought it a shame for him to be idle. Moreover, he did not blunder unconsciously upon his triumph; he tackled the trade in so fine a spirit of analysis that he might have been the very Aristotle of his science. "The keek-cloy," he wrote, in his hints to young sportsmen, "is easily picked. If the notes are in the long fold, just tip them the forks; but if there is a purse or open money in the case, you must link it." The breast-pocket, on the other hand, is a severer test. "Picking the suck is sometimes a kittle job," again the philosopher speaks. "If the coat is buttoned it must be opened by slipping past. Then bring the lil down between the flap of the coat and the body, keeping your spare arm across your man's breast, and so slip it to a comrade; then abuse the fellow for jostling you."

But not only did he master the tradition of thievery; he vaunted his originality with the familiar complacence of the scoundrel. Forgetting that it was by burglary that he was undone, he explains for his public glorification that he was wont to enter the houses of Leith by forcing the small window above the outer door. This artifice, his vanity grumbles, is now common; but he would have all the world understand that it was his own invention, and he murmurs with the priggishness of the convicted criminal that it is now set forth for the better protection of honest citizens. No less admirable in his own eyes was that other artifice which induced him to conceal such notes as he managed to filch in the collar of his coat. Thus he eluded the vigilance of the police, which searched its prey in those days with a sorry lack of cunning. But, in truth, Haggart's wits were as nimble as his fingers, and he seldom failed to render a profitable account of his talents. He beguiled one of his many sojourns in gaol by manufacturing tinder wherewith to light the prisoners' pipes, and it is not astonishing that he won an instant popularity. In Ireland, when the constables would take him for a Scot, he answered in high Tipperary, and saved his skin for a while by a brogue which would not have shamed a modern patriot. But quick as were his wits, his vanity always outstripped them, and no hero ever bragged of his achievements with a louder effrontery.

Now all you ramblers in mourning go, For the prince of ramblers is lying low, And all you maidens that love the game, Put on your mourning veils again.

Thus he celebrated his downfall in a ballad that has the true Newgate ring, and verily in his own eyes he was a hero who carried to the scaffold a dauntless spirit unstained by treachery.

He believed himself an adept in all the arts; as a squire of dames he held himself peerless, and he assured the ineffable Combe, who recorded his flippant utterance with a credulous respect, that he had sacrificed hecatombs of innocent virgins to his importunate lust. Prose and verse trickled with equal facility from his pen, and his biography is a masterpiece. Written in the pedlar's French as it was mis-spoken in the hells of Edinburgh, it is a narrative of uncommon simplicity and directness, marred now and again by such superfluous reflections as are the natural result of thievish sentimentality. He tells his tale without paraphrase or adornment, and the worthy Writer to the Signet, who prepared the work for the Press, would have asked three times the space to record one-half the adventures. "I sunk upon it with my forks and brought it with me"; "We obtained thirty-three pounds by this affair"—is there not the stalwart flavour of the epic in these plain, unvarnished sentences?

But his other accomplishments are pallid in the light of his brilliant left hand. Once, at Derry—he attended a cock-fight, and beguiled an interval by emptying the pockets of a lucky bookmaker. An expert, who watched the exploit in admiration, could not withhold a compliment. "You are the Switcher," he exclaimed; "some take all, but you leave nothing." And it is as the Switcher that Haggart keeps his memory green.

II
GENTLEMAN HARRY

"DAMN ye both! stop, or I will blow your brains out!" Thus it was that Harry Simms greeted his victims, proving in a phrase that the heroic age of the rumpad was no more. Forgotten the debonair courtesy of Claude Duval! Forgotten the lightning wit, the swift repartee of the incomparable Hind! No longer was the hightoby-gloak a "gentleman" of the road; he was a butcher, if not a beggar, on horseback; a braggart without the courage to pull a trigger; a swashbuckler, oblivious of that ancient style which converted the misery of surrender into a privilege. Yet Harry Simms, the supreme adventurer of his age, was not without distinction; his lithe form and his hard-ridden horse were the common dread of England; his activity was rewarded with a princely treasure; and if his method were lacking in urbanity, the excuse is that he danced not to the brilliant measure of the Cavaliers, but limped to the clumsy fiddle-scraping of the early Georges.

At Eton, where a too-indulgent grandmother had placed him, he ransacked the desks of his schoolfellows, and avenged a birching by emptying his master's pockets. Wherefore he lost the hope of a polite education, and instead of proceeding with a clerkly dignity to King's College, in the University of Cambridge, he was ignomini- ously apprenticed to a breeches-maker. But the one restraint was as irksome as the other, and Harry Simms abandoned the needle, as he had scorned the grammar, to go upon the pad. Though his early companions were scragged at Tyburn the light- fingered rascal was indifferent to their fate, and squandering such booty as fell to his share, he bravely "turned out" for more. Tottenham Court Fair was the theatre of his childish exploits, and there he gained some little skill in the picking of pockets. But a spell of bad trade brought him to poverty, and he attempted to replenish an empty pocket by the childish expedient of a threatening letter.

The plan was conceived and executed with a futility which ensured an instant capture. The bungler chose a stranger at haphazard, commanding him, under pen- alty of death, to lay five guineas upon a gun in Tower Wharf; the guineas were cun- ningly deposited, and the rascal, caught with his hand upon the booty, was commit- ted to Newgate. Youth, and the intercession of his grandmother, procured a release, unjustified by the infamous stupidity of the trick. Its very clumsiness should have sent him over sea; and it is wonderful that from a beginning of so little promise, he should have climbed even the first slopes of greatness. However, the memory of gaol forced him to a brief interlude of honesty; for a while he wore the pink coat of Colonel Cunningham's postillion, and presently was promoted to the independence of a hackney coach.

Thus employed, he became acquainted with the famous Cyprians of Covent Garden, who, loving him for his handsome face and sprightly gesture, seduced him to desert his cab for an easier profession. So long as the sky was fair, he lived under their amiable protection; but the summer having chased the smarter gentry from town, the ladies could afford him no more than would purchase a horse and a pair of pistols, so that Harry was compelled to challenge fortune on the high road. His first journey was triumphantly successful. A post-chaise and a couple of coaches emptied their wealth into his hands, and, riding for London, he was able to return the favours lavished upon him by Covent Garden. At the first touch of gold he was transformed to a finished blade. He purchased himself a silver-hiked sword, which he dangled over a discreet suit of black velvet; a prodigious run of luck at the gaming-tables kept his purse well lined; and he made so brilliant an appearance in his familiar haunts that he speedily gained the name of "Gentleman Harry." But the money, lightly won, was lightly spent. The tables took back more than they gave, and before long Simms was astride his horse again, flourishing his irons, and crying: "Stand and deliver"! upon every road in England.

Epping Forest was his general hunting-ground, but his enterprise took him far afield, and if one night he galloped by starlight across Bagshot Heath, another he was holding up the York stage with unbridled insolence. He robbed, he roared, he blustered with praiseworthy industry; and good luck coming to the aid of caution, he escaped for a while the necessary punishment of his crimes. It was on Stockbridge Downs that he met his first check. He had stopped a chariot, and came off with a hatful of gold, but the victims, impatient of disaster, raised the county, and Gentleman Harry was laid by the heels. Never at a loss, he condescended to a cringing hypocrisy: he whined, he whimpered, he babbled of reform, he plied his prosecutors with letters so packed with penitence, that they abandoned their case, and in a couple of days Simms had eased a collector at Eversey Bank of three hundred pounds. For this enterprise two others climbed the gallows, and the robber's pride in his capture was miserably lessened by the shedding of innocent blood.

But he forgot his remorse as speedily as he dissipated his money, and sentimentality neither damped his enjoyment nor restrained his energy. Even his brief visits to London were turned to the best account; and, though he would have the world believe him a mere voluptuary, his eye was bent sternly upon business. If he did lose his money in a gambling hell, he knew who won it, and spoke with his opponent on the homeward way. In his eyes a fuddled rake was always fair game, and the stern windows of St. Clement's Church looked down upon many a profitable adventure. His most distinguished journey was to Ireland, whither he set forth to find a market for his stolen treasure. But he determined that the road should bear its own charges, and he reached Dublin a richer man than he left London. In three months he was penniless, but he did not begin trade again until he had recrossed the Channel, and, having got to work near Chester, he returned to the Piazza fat with bank-notes.

With success, his extravagance increased, and, living the life of a man about town, he was soon harassed by debt. More than once he was lodged in the Marshalsea, and as his violent temper resented the interference of a dun, he became notorious for his assaults upon sheriff's officers. And thus his poor skill grew poorer: forgetting his trade, he expected that brandy would ease his embarrassment. At last, sodden with drink, he enlisted in the Guards, from which regiment he deserted, only to be pressed aboard a man-of-war. Freed by a clever trick, he took to the road again, until a paltry theft from a barber transported him to Maryland. There he turned sailor, and his ship, *The Two Sisters,* being taken by a privateer, he contrived to scramble into Portugal, whence he made his way back to England, and to the only adventure of which he was master. He landed with no more money than the price of a pistol, but he prigged a prancer at Bristol horsefair, and set out upon his last journey. The tide of his fortune was at flood. He crammed his pockets with watches; he was owner of enough diamonds to set up shop in a fashionable quarter; of guineas he had as many as would support his magnificence for half a year; and at last he resolved to quit the road, and to live like the gentleman he was. To this prudence he was the more easily persuaded, because not only were the thief-takers eager for his capture, but he was a double-dyed deserter, whose sole chance of quietude was a decent obscurity. His resolution was taken at St. Albans, and over a comfortable dinner he pictured a serene and uneventful future. On the morrow he would set forth to Dublin, sell his handsome stock of jewels, and forget that the cart ever lumbered up Tyburn Hill. So elated was he with his growing virtue, that he called for a second bottle, and as the port heated his blood his fingers tingled for action. A third bottle proved beyond dispute that only the craven were idle; "and why," he exclaimed, generous with wine, "should the most industrious ruffler of England condescend to inaction?" Instantly he summoned the ostler, screaming for his horse, and before Redburn he had emptied four pockets, and had exchanged his own tired jade for a fresh and willing beast. Still exultant in his contempt of cowardice, he faced the Warrington stage, and made off with his plunder at a drunken gallop. Arrived at Dunstable, he was so befogged with liquor and pride, that he entered the "Bull Inn," the goal of the very coach he had just encountered. He had scarce called for a quartern of brandy when the robbed passengers thronged into the kitchen; and the fright gave him enough sobriety to leave his glass untasted, and stagger to his horse. In a wild fury of arrogance and terror, of conflicting vice and virtue, he pressed on to Hockcliffe, where he took refuge from the rain, and presently, fuddled with more brandy, he fell asleep over the kitchen fire.

But by this time the hue and cry was raised; and as the hero lay helpless in the corner three troopers burst into the inn, levelled their pistols at his head, and threatened instant death if he put his hand to his pocket. Half asleep, and wholly drunk, he made not the smallest show of resistance; he surrendered all his money, watches, and diamonds, save a little that was sewn into his neckcloth, and sulkily crawled up to his bed-chamber. Thither the troopers followed him, and having restored some nine pounds at his urgent demand, they watched his heavy slumbers. For all his brandy Simms slept but uneasily, and awoke in the night sick with the remorse which is bred of ruined plans and a splitting head. He got up wearily, and sat over the fire "a good deal chagrined," to quote his own simple phrase, at his miserable capture. Escape seemed hopeless indeed; there crouched the vigilant troopers, scowling on their prey. A thousand plans chased each other through the hero's fuddled brain, and at last he resolved to tempt the cupidity of his guardians, and to make himself master of their fire-arms. There were still left him a couple of seals, one gold, the other silver, and, watching his opportunity, Simms flung them with a flourish in the fire. It fell out as he expected; the hungry troopers made a dash to save the trinkets; the prisoner seized a brace of pistols and leapt to the door. But, alas, the pistols missed fire, Harry was immediately overpowered, and on the morrow was carried, sick and sorry, before the Justice. From Dunstable he travelled his last journey to Newgate, and, being condemned at the Old Bailey, he was hanged till he was dead, and his body thereafter was carried for dissection to a surgeon's in that same Co vent Garden where he first deserted his hackney cab for the pleasures of the town.

"Gentleman Harry" was neither a brilliant thief nor a courteous highwayman. There was no touch of the grand manner even in his prettiest achievement. His predecessors had made a pistol and a vizard an overwhelming terror, and he did but profit by their tradition when he bade the cowed traveller stand and deliver. His profession, as he practised it, neither demanded skill nor incurred danger. Though he threatened death at every encounter, you never hear that he pulled a trigger throughout his career. If his opponent jeered and rode off, he rode off with a whole skin and a full pocket. Once even this renowned adventurer accepted the cut of a riding-whip across his face, nor made any attempt to avenge the insult. But his manifold shortcomings were no hindrance to his success. Wherever he went, between London and York, he stopped coaches and levied his tax. A threatening voice, an arched eyebrow, an arrogant method of fingering an unloaded pistol, conspired with the craven, indolent habit of the time to make his every journey a procession of triumph. He was capable of performing all such feats as the age required of him. But you miss the spirit, the bravery, the urbanity, and the wit, which made the adventurer of the seventeenth century a figure of romance.

One point only of the great tradition did Harry Simms remember. He was never unwilling to restore a trinket made precious by sentiment. Once when he took a gold ring from a gentleman's finger, a gentlewoman burst into tears, exclaiming, "There goes your father's ring." Whereupon Simms threw all his booty into a hat, saying, "For God's sake, take that or anything else you please." But in all other respects he was a bully, with the hesitancy of a coward, rather than the proper rival of Hind or Duval. Apart from the exercise of his trade, he was a very Mohock for brutality. He would ill-treat his victims, whenever their drunkenness permitted the freedom, and he had no better gifts for the women who were kind to him than cruelty and neglect. One of his many imprisonments was the result of a monstrous ferocity. "Unluckily in a quarrel," he tells you gravely, "I ran a crab-stick into a woman's eye"; and well did he deserve his sojourn in the New Prison. At another time he rewarded the keeper of a coffee-house, who supported him for six months, by stealing her watch; and, when she grumbled at his insolence, he reflected, with a chuckle, that she could more easily bear the loss of her watch than the loss of her lover. Even in his gaiety there was an unpleasant spice of greed and truculence. Once, when he was still seen in fashionable company, he went to a masquerade, dressed in a rich Spanish habit, lent him by a Captain in the Guards, and he made so fine a show that he captivated a young and beautiful Cyprian, whom, when she would have treated him with generosity, he did but reward with the loss of all her jewels.

Moreover, he had so small a regard for his craft, that he would spoil his effects by drink or debauchery; and, though a highwayman, he cared so little for style, that he would as lief trick a drunken gamester as face his man on Bagshot Heath or beneath the shade of Epping Forest. You admire not his success, because, like the success of the popular politician, it depended rather upon his dupes than upon his merit. You approve not his raffish exploits in the hells of Covent Garden or Drury Lane. But you cannot withhold respect from his consistent dandyism, and you are grateful for the record that, engaged in a mean enterprise, he was dressed "in a green velvet frock and a short lac'd waistcoat." Above all, his picturesque capture at Hockcliffe, atones for much stupidity. The resolution, wavering at the wine-glass, the last drunken ride from St. Albans—these are inventions in experience, which should make Simms immortal. And when he sits "by the fireside a good deal chagrined," he recalls the arrest of a far greater man—even of Cartouche, who was surprised by the soldiers at his bedside stitching a torn pair of breeches. His auto-biography, wherein "he relates the truth as a dying man," seemed excellent in the eyes of Borrow, who loved it so well that he imagined a sentence, ascribed it falsely to Simms, and then rewarded it with extravagant applause. But Gentleman Harrfy knew how to tell a simple story, and the book, "all wrote by myself while under sentence of death," is his best performance. In action he had many faults, for, if he was a highwayman among rakes, he was but a rake among highwaymen.

III
A PARALLEL

(THE SWITCHER AND GENTLEMAN HARRY)

HAGGART and Simms are united in the praise of Borrow, and in the generous applause of posterity. Each resumes for his own generation the prowess of his kind. Each has assured his immortality by an experiment in literature; and if epic simplicity and rapid narrative are the virtues of biography, it is difficult to award the prize. The Switcher preferred to write in the rough lingo, wherein he best expressed himself. He packs his pages with ill-spelt slang, telling his story of thievery in the true language of thieves. Gentleman Harry, as became a person of quality, mimicked the dialect wherewith he was familiar in the more fashionable gambling dens of Covent Garden. Both write without the smallest suggestion of false shame or idle regret, and a natural vanity lifts each of them out of the pit of commonplace on to the tableland of the heroic. They set forth their depredation, as a victorious general might record his triumphs, and they excel the nimblest Ordinary that ever penned a dying speech in all the gifts of the historian.

But when you leave the study for the field, the Switcher instantly declares his superiority. He had the happiness to practise his craft in its heyday, while Simms knew but the fag-end of a noble tradition. Haggart, moreover, was an expert, pursuing a difficult art, while Simms was a bully, plundering his betters by bluff. Simms boasted no quality which might be set off against the accurate delicacy of Haggart's hand. The Englishman grew rich upon a rolling eye and a rusty pistol. He put on his "fiercest manner," and believed that the world would deny him nothing. The Scot, rejoicing in his exquisite skill, went to work without fuss or bluster, and added the joy of artistic pride to his delight in plunder. Though Simms's manner seems the more chivalrous, it required not one tithe of the courage which was Haggart's necessity. On horseback, with the semblance of a fire-arm, a man may easily challenge a coachful of women. It needs a cool brain and sound courage to empty a pocket in the watchful presence of spies and policemen. While Gentleman Harry chose a lonely road, or the cover of night for his exploits, the Switcher always worked by day, hustled by a crowd of witnesses.

Their hours of leisure furnish a yet more striking contrast. Simms was a polished dandy delighting in his clothes, unhappy if he were deprived of his bottle and his game. Haggart, on the other hand, was before all things sealed to his profession. He would have deserted the gayest masquerade, had he ever strayed into so light a frivolity, for the chance of lightening a pocket. He tasted but few amusements without the limits of his craft, and he preserved unto the end a touch of that dour character which is the heritage of his race. But, withal, he was an amiable, decent body, who would have recoiled in horror from the drunken brutality of Gentleman Harry. Though he bragged to George Combe of his pitiless undoing of wenches, he never thrust a crab-stick into a woman's eye, and he was incapable of rewarding a kindness by robbery and neglect. Once—at Newcastle—he arrayed himself in a smart white coat and tops, but the splendour ill became his red-headed awkwardness, and he would have stood aghast at the satin frocks and velvet waistcoats of him who broke the hearts of Drury Lane. But if he were gentler in his life, Haggart was prepared to fight with a more reckless courage when his trade demanded it. It was the Gentleman's boast that he never shed the blood of man. But when David found a turnkey between himself and freedom, he did not hesitate to kill, though his remorse was bitter enough when he neared the gallows. In brief, Haggart was not only the better craftsman, but the honester fellow, and though his hands were red with blood, he deserved his death far less than did the more truculent, less valiant Simms. Each had in his brain the stuff whereof men of letters are made: this is their parallel. And, by way of contrast, while the Switcher was an accomplished artist, Gentleman Harry was a roystering braggart.

DEACON BRODIE AND CHARLES PEACE
I
DEACON BRODIE

AS William Brodie stood at the bar, on trial for his life, he seemed the gallantest gentleman in court. Thither he had been carried in a chair, and, still conscious of the honour paid him, he flashed a condescending smile upon his judges. His step was jaunty as ever; his superb attire well became the Deacon of a Guild. His coat was blue, his vest a very garden of flowers; while his satin breeches and his stockings of white silk were splendid in their simplicity. Beneath a cocked hat his hair was fully dressed and powdered, and even the prosecuting counsel assailed him with the respect due to a man of fashion. The fellow's magnificence was thrown into relief by the squalor of his accomplice. For George Smith had neither the money nor the taste to habit himself as a polished rogue, and he huddled as far from his master as he could in the rags of his mean estate. Nor from this moment did Brodie ever abate one jot of his dignity. He faced his accusers with a clear eye and a frigid amiability; he listened to his sentence with a calm contempt; he laughed complacently at the sorry interludes of judicial wit; and he faced the last music with a bravery and a cynicism which bore the stamp of true greatness.

It was not until after his crime that Brodie's heroism approved itself. And even then his was a triumph not of skill but of character. Always a gentleman in manner and conduct, he owed the success and the failure of his life to this one quality. When in flight he made for Flushing on board the *Endeavour,* the other passengers, who knew not his name, straightway christened him "the gentleman." The enterprise itself would have been impossible to one less persuasively gifted, and its proper execution is a tribute to the lofty quality of his mind. There was he in London, a stranger and a fugitive; yet instead of crawling furtively into a coal-barge he charters a ship, captures the confidence of the captain, carries the other passengers to Flushing, when they were bound for Leith, and compels every one to confess his charm! The thief, also, found him irresistible; and while the game lasted, the flash kens of Edinburgh murmured the Deacon's name in the hushed whisper of respect.

His fine temperament disarmed treachery. In London he visited an ancient doxy of his own, who, with her bully, shielded him from justice, though betrayal would have met with an ample reward. Smith, if he knew himself the superior craftsman, trembled at the Deacon's nod, who thus swaggered it through life, with none to withhold the exacted reverence. To this same personal compulsion he owed his worldly advancement. Deacon of the Wrights' Guild while still a young man, he served upon the Council, was known for one of Edinburgh's honoured citizens, and never went abroad unmarked by the finger of respectful envy. He was elected in 1773 a member of the Cape Club, and met at the Isle of Man Arms in Craig's Close the wittiest men of his time and town. Raeburn, Runciman, and Ferguson the poet, were of the society, and it was with such men as these that Brodie might have wasted his vacant hour. Indeed, at the very moment that he was cracking cribs and shaking the ivories, he was a chosen leader of fashion and gaiety; and it was the elegance of the "gentleman" that distinguished him from his fellows.

The fop, indeed, had climbed the altitudes of life; the cracksman still stumbled in the valleys. If he had a ready cunning in the planning of an enterprise, he must needs bungle at the execution$ and had he not been associated with George Smith, a king of scoundrels, there would be few exploits to record. And yet for the craft of housebreaker he had one solid advantage: he knew the locks and bolts of Edinburgh as he knew his primer—for had he not fashioned the most of them himself? But, his knowledge once imparted to his accomplices, he cheerfully sank to a menial's office. In no job did he play a principal's part: he was merely told off by Smith or another to guard the entrance and sound the alarm. When McKain's on the Bridge was broken, the Deacon found the false keys; but it was Smith who carried off such poor booty as was found. And though the master suggested the attack upon Brace's shop, knowing full well the simplicity of the lock, he lingered at the Vintner's over a game of hazard, and let the man pouch a sumptuous booty.

Even the onslaught upon the Excise Office, which cost his life, was contrived with appalling clumsiness. The Deacon of the Wrights' Guild, who could slash wood at his will, who knew the artifice of every lock in the city, let his men go to work with no better implements than the stolen coulter of a plough and a pair of spurs. And when they tackled the ill-omened job, Brodie was of those who brought failure upon it. Long had they watched the door of the Excise; long had they studied the habits of its clerks; so that they went to work in no vain spirit of experiment. Nor on the fatal night did they force an entrance until they had dogged the porter to his home. Smith and Brown ransacked for money, while Brodie and Andrew Ainslie remained without to give a necessary warning. Whereupon Ainslie was seized with fright, and Brodie, losing his head, called off the others, so that six hundred pounds were left, that might have been an easy prey. Smith, indignant at the collapse of the long-pondered design, laid the blame upon his master, and they swung, as Brodie's grim spirit of farce suggested, for four pounds apiece.

But the humours of the situation were all the Deacon's own. He dressed the part in black; his respectability grinned behind a vizard; and all the while he trifled nonchalantly with a pistol. Breaking the silence with snatches from *The Beggar's Opera,* he promised that all their lead should turn to gold, christened the coulter and the crow the Great and Little Samuel, and then went off to drink and dice at the Vintner's. How could anger prevail against this undying gaiety? And if Smith were peevish at failure, he was presently reconciled, and prepared once mote to die for his Deacon.

Even after escape, the amateur is still apparent. True, he managed the trip to Flushing with his ancient extravagance; true, he employed all the juggleries of the law to prevent his surrender at Amsterdam. But he knew not the caution of the born criminal, and he was run to earth, because he would still write to his friends like a gentleman. His letters, during this nightmare of disaster, are perfect in their carelessness and good-fellowship. In this he demands news of his children, as becomes a father and a citizen, and furnishes a schedule of their education; in that he is curious concerning the issue of a main, and would know whether his black cock came off triumphant. Nor, even in flight, did he forget his proper craft, but would have his tools sent to Charleston, that in America he might resume the trade that had made him Deacon.

But his was the art of conduct, not of guile, and he deserved capture for his rare indifference. Why, then, with no natural impulsion, did he risk the gallows? Why, being no born thief, and innocent of the thief's cunning, did he associate with so clever a scoundrel as George Smith, with cowards craven as Brown and Ainslie? The greed of gold, doubtless, half persuaded him, but gold was otherwise attainable, and the motive was assuredly far more subtle. Brodie, in fact, was of a romantic turn. He was, so to say, a glorified schoolboy, surfeited with penny dreadfuls. He loved above all things to patter the flash, to dream himself another Macheath, to trick himself out with all the trappings of a crime he was unfit to commit. It was never the job itself that attracted him: he would always rather throw the dice than force a neighbour's window. But he must needs have a distraction from the respectability of his life. Everybody was at his feet; he was Deacon of his Guild, at an age whereat his fellows were striving to earn a reputable living; his masterpieces were fashioned, and the wrights' trade was already a burden. To go upon the cross seemed a dream of freedom, until he snapped his fingers at the world, filled his mouth with slang, prepared his *alibi,* and furnished him a whole wardrobe of disguises.

With a conscious irony, maybe, he buried his pistols beneath the domestic hearth, jammed his dark lantern into the press, where he kept his game-cocks, and determined to make an inextricable jumble of his career. Drink is sometimes a sufficient reaction against the orderliness of a successful life. But drink and cards failed with the Deacon, and at the Vintner's of his frequentation he encountered accomplices proper for his schemes. Never was so outrageous a protest offered against domesticity. Yet Brodie's resolution was romantic after its fashion, and was far more respectable than the blackguardism of the French Revolution, which distracted housewifely discontent a year after the Deacon swung. Moreover, it gave occasion for his dandyism and his love of display. If in one incarnation he was the complete gentleman, in another he dressed the part of the perfect scoundrel, and the list of his costumes would have filled one of his own ledgers.

But, when once the possibility of housebreaking was taken from him, he returned to his familiar dignity. Being questioned by the Procurator Fiscal, he shrugged his shoulders, regretting that other affairs demanded his attention. As who should say: it is unpardonable to disturb the meditations of a gentleman. He made a will bequeathing his knowledge of law to the magistrates of Edinburgh, his dexterity in cards and dice to Hamilton the chimney-sweeper, and all his bad qualities to his good friends and old companions, Brown and Ainslie, not doubting, however, that their own will secure them a "rope at last." In prison it was his worst complaint that, though the nails of his toes and fingers were not quite so long as Nebuchadnezzar's, they were long enough for a mandarin, and much longer than he found convenient. Thus he pre served an untroubled demeanour until the day of his death. Always polite, and even joyous, he met the smallest indulgence with enthusiasm. When Smith complained that a respite of six weeks was of small account, Brodie exclaimed, "George, what would you and I give for six weeks longer? Six weeks would be an age to us."

But the day of execution was the day of his supreme triumph. As some men are artists in their lives, so the Deacon was an artist in his death. Nothing became him so well as his manner of leaving the world. There is never a blot upon this exquisite performance. It is superb, impeccable! Again his dandyism supported him, and he played the part of a dying man in a full suit of black, his hair, as always, dressed and powdered. The day before he had been jovial and sparkling. He had chanted all his flash songs, and cracked the jokes of a man of fashion. But he set out for the gallows with a firm step and a rigorous demeanour. He offered a prayer of his own composing, and "O Lord," he said, "I lament that I know so little of Thee." The patronage and the confession are alike characteristic. As he drew near the scaffold, the model of which he had given to his native city a few years since, he stepped with an agile briskness; he examined the halter, destined for his neck, with an impartial curiosity.

His last pleasantry was uttered as he ascended the table. "George," he muttered, a you are first in hand," and thereafter he took farewell of his friends. Only one word of petulance escaped his lips: when the halters were found too short, his contempt for slovenly workmanship urged him to protest, and to demand a punishment for the executioner. But again ascending the table, he assured himself against further mishap by arranging the rope with his own hands. Thus he was turned off in a brilliant assembly. The Provost and Magistrates, in respect for his dandyism, were resplendent in their robes of office, and though the crowd of spectators rivalled that which paid a tardy honour to Jonathan Wild, no one was hurt except the customary policeman. Such was the dignified end of a "double life." And the duplicity is the stranger, because the real Deacon was not Brodie the Cracksman, but Brodie the Gentleman. So lightly did he esteem life that he tossed it from him in a careless impulse. So little did he fear death that, "What is hanging?" he asked. "A leap in the dark."

II
CHARLES PEACE

CHARLES PEACE, after the habit of his kind, was born of scrupulously honest parents. The son of a religious file-maker, he owed to his father not only his singular piety but his love of edged tools. As he never encountered an iron bar whose scission baffled him, so there never was a fire-eating Methodist to whose ministrations he would not turn a repentant ear. After a handy portico and a rich booty he loved nothing so well as a soul-stirring discourse. Not even his precious fiddle occupied a larger space in his heart than that devotion which the ignorant have termed hypocrisy. Wherefore his career was no less suitable to his ambition than his inglorious end. For he lived the king of housebreakers, and he died a warning to all evildoers, with a prayer of intercession trembling upon his lips.

The hero's boyhood is wrapped in obscurity. But it is certain that no glittering precocity brought disappointment to his maturer years, and he was already nineteen when he achieved his first imprisonment. Even then 'twas a sorry offence, which merited no more than a month, so that he returned to freedom and his fiddle with his character unbesmirched. Serious as ever in pious exercises, he gained a scanty living as strolling musician. There was never a tavern in Sheffield where the twang of his violin was unheard, and the skill wherewith he extorted music from a single string earned him the style and title of the modern Paganini. But such an employ was too mean for his pride, and he soon got to work again—this time with a better success. The mansions of Sheffield were his early prey, and a rich plunder rewarded his intrepidity. The design was as masterly as its accomplishment. The grand style is already discernible. The houses were broken in quietude and good order. None saw the opened window; none heard the step upon the stair; in truth, the victim's loss was his first intelligence.

But when the booty was in the robber's own safe keeping, the empiricism of his method was revealed. As yet he knew no secret and efficient fence to shield him from detection; as yet he had not learnt that the complete burglar works alone. This time he knew two accomplices—women both, and one his own sister! A paltry pair of boots was the clue of discovery, and a goodly stretch was the proper reward of a clumsy indiscretion. So for twenty years he wavered between the crowbar and the prison-house, now perfecting a brilliant scheme, now captured through reckless-ness or drink. Once when a mistake at Manchester sent him to the Hulks, he owned his failure was the fruit of brandy, and after his wont delivered (from the dock) a little homily upon the benefit of sobriety.

Meanwhile his art was growing to perfection. He had at last discovered that a burglary demands as diligent a forethought as a campaign; he had learnt that no great work is achieved by a multitude of minds. Before his boat carried off a goodly parcel of silk from Nottingham, he was known to the neighbourhood as an enthu-siastic and skilful angler. One day he dangled his line, the next he sat peacefully at the same employ; and none suspected that the mild-mannered fisherman had under the cloud of night despatched a costly parcel to London. Even the years of imprison-ment were not ill-spent. Peace was still preparing the great achievement of his life, and he framed from solitary reflection as well as from his colleagues in crime many an ingenious theory afterwards fearlessly translated into practice. And when at last he escaped the slavery of the gaol, picture-framing was the pursuit which covered the sterner business of his life. His depredation involved him in no suspicion; his changing features rendered recognition impossible. When the exercise of his trade compelled him to shoot a policeman at Whalley Range, another was sentenced for the crime; and had he not encountered Mrs. Dyson, who knows but he might have practised his art in prosperous obscurity until claimed by a coward's death? But a stormy love-passage with Mrs. Dyson led to the unworthy killing of the woman's husband—a crime unnecessary and in no sense consonant to the burglar's craft; and Charles Peace was an outlaw, with a reward set upon his head.

And now came a period of true splendour. Like Fielding, like Cervantes, like Sterne, Peace reserved his veritable masterpiece for the certainty of middle-life. His last two years were nothing less than a march of triumph. If you remember his constant danger, you will realise the grandeur of the scheme. From the moment that Peace left Bannercross with Dyson's blood upon his hands, he was a hunted man. His capture was worth five hundred pounds; his features were familiar to a hundred hungry detectives. Had he been: less than a man of genius, he might have taken an unavailing refuge in flight or concealment. But, content with no safety unattended by affluence, he devised a surer plan: he became a householder. Now, a semidetached villa is an impregnable stronghold. Respectability oozes from the dusky mortar of its bricks, and escapes in clouds of smoke from its soot-grimed chimneys. No policeman ever detects a desperate ruffian. in a demure black-coated gentleman who day after day turns an iron gate upon its rusty hinge. And thus, wrapt in a cloak of suburban piety, Peace waged a, pitiless and effective war upon his neighbours.

He pillaged Blackheath, Greenwich, Peckham, and. many another home of honest worthy with a noiselessnes and a precision that were the envy of the whole family. The unknown and intrepid burglar was a terror to all the clerkdom of the City, and though he was as secret and secluded as Peace, the two heroes were never identified. At the time of his true eminence he a "resided" in Evelina Road, Peckham, and none was more sensible than he how well the address became his provincial refinement. There he installed himself with his wife and Mrs. Thompson. His drawing-room suite was the envy of the neighbourhood; his pony trap proclaimed him a man of substance; his gentle manners won the respect of all Peckham. Hither he would invite his friends to such entertainments as the suburb expected. His musical evenings were recorded in the local paper, while on Sundays he chanted the songs of Zion with a zeal which Clapham herself might envy.

But the house in Evelina Road was no mere haunt of quiet gentility. It was chosen with admirable forethought and with a stern eye upon the necessities of business. Beyond the garden wall frowned a railway embankment, which enabled the cracksman to escape from his house without opening the front door. By the same embankment he might, if he chose, convey the trophies of the night's work; and what mattered it if the windows rattled to the passing train? At least a cloud of suspicion was dispelled. Here he lived for two years, with naught to disturb his tranquility save Mrs. Thompson's taste for drink. The hours of darkness were spent in laborious activity, the open day brought its own distractions. There was always

Bow Street wherein to loaf, and the study of the criminal law lost none of its excitement from the reward offered outside for the bald-headed fanatic who sat placidly within. And the love of music was Peace's constant solace. Whatever treasures he might discard in a hurried flight, he never left a fiddle behind, and so vast became his pilfered collection that he had to borrow an empty room in a friend's house for its better disposal.

Moreover, he had a fervent pride in his craft; and you might deduce from his performance the whole theory and practice of burglary. He worked ever without accomplices. He knew neither the professional thief nor his lingo; and no association with gaol-birds involved him in the risk of treachery and betrayal. His single colleague was a friendly fence, and not even at the gallow's foot would he surrender this fence's name. But his master quality was a constructive imagination. Accident never marred his design. He would visit the house of his breaking until he understood its ground-plan, and was familiar with its inhabitants. This demanded an amazing circumspection, but Peace was as stealthy as a cat, and he would keep silent vigil for hours rather than fail from a too instant anxiety. Having marked the place of his entry, and having chosen an appropriate hour, he would prevent the egress of his enemies by screwing up the doors. He then secured the room wherein he worked, and, the job finished, he slung himself into the night by the window, so that, ere an alarm could be raised, his pony-trap had carried the booty to Evelina Road.

Such was the outline of his plan; but, being no pedant, he varied it at will: nor was he likely to court defeat through lack of resource. Accomplished as he was in his proper business, he was equally alert to meet the accompanying risks. He had brought the art of cozening strange dogs to perfection; and for the exigence of escape, his physical equipment was complete. He would resist capture with unparalleled determination, and though he shuddered at the shedding of blood, he never hesitated when necessity bade him pull the trigger. Moreover, there was no space into which he would not squeeze his body, and the iron bars were not yet devised through which he could not make an exit. Once—it was at Nottingham—he was surprised by an inquisitive detective who demanded his name and trade. "I am a hawker of spectacles," replied Peace, "and my licence is downstairs. Wait two. minutes and I'll show it you." The detective never saw him again. Six inches only separated the bars of the window, but Peace asked no more, and thus silently he won his freedom. True, his most daring feat—the leap from the train—resulted not in liberty, but in a broken head. But he essayed a task too high even for his endeavour, and, despite his manacles, at least he left his boot in the astonished warder's grip.

No less remarkable than his skill and daring were his means of evasion. Even without a formal disguise he could elude pursuit. At an instant's warning, his loose, plastic features would assume another shape; out shot his lower jaw, and, as if by magic, the blood flew into his face until you might take him for a mulatto. Or, if he chose, he would strap his arm to his side, and let the police be baffled by a wooden mechanism decently finished with a hook. Thus he roamed London up and down unsuspected, and even after his last failure at Blackheath, none would have discovered Charles Peace in John Ward, the Single-Handed Burglar, had not woman's treachery prompted detection. Indeed, he was an epitome of his craft, the Complete Burglar made manifest.

Not only did he plan his victories with previous ingenuity, but he sacrificed to his success both taste and sentiment. His dress was always of the most sombre; his only wear was the decent black of everyday godliness. The least spice of dandyism might have distinguished him from his fellows, and Peace's whole vanity lay in his craft. Nor did the paltty sentiment of friendship deter him from his just course. When the panic aroused by the silent burglar was uncontrolled, a neighbour consulted Peace concerning the safety of his house. The robber, having duly noted the villa's imperfections, and having discovered the hiding-place of jewellery and plate, complacently rifled it the next night. Though his self-esteem sustained a shock, though henceforth his friend thought meanly of his judgment, he was rewarded with the solid pudding of plunder, and the world whispered of the mysterious marauder with a yet colder horror. In truth, the large simplicity and solitude of his style sets him among the Classics, and though others have surpassed him at single points of the game, he practised the art with such universal breadth and courage as were then a revolution, and are still unsurpassed.

But the burglar ever fights an unequal battle. One false step, and defeat o'erwhelms him. For two years had John Ward intimidated the middle-class seclusion of South London; for two years had he hidden from a curious world the ugly, furrowed visage of Charles Peace. The bald head, the broad-rimmed spectacles, the squat, thick figure—he stood but five feet four in his stockings, and adds yet another to the list of little-great men—should have ensured detection, but the quick change and the persuasive gesture were omnipotent, and until the autumn of 1878 Peace was comfortably at large. And then an encounter at Blackheath put him within the clutch of justice. His revolver failed in its duty, and, valiant as he was, at last he met his match. In prison he was alternately insolent and aggrieved. He blustered for justice, proclaimed himself the victim of sudden temptation, and insisted that his intention had been ever innocent.

But, none the less, he was sentenced to a lifer, and, the mask of John Ward being torn from him, he was sent to Sheffield to stand his trial as Charles Peace. The leap from the train is already recorded; and at his last appearance in the dock he rolled upon the floor, a petulant and broken man. When once the last doom was pronounced, he forgot both fiddle and crowbar; he surrendered himself to those exercises of piety from which he had never wavered. The foolish have denounced him for a hypocrite, not knowing that the artist may have a life apart from his art, and that to Peace religion was an essential pursuit. So he died, having released from an unjust sentence the poor wretch who at Whalley Range had suffered for his crime, and offering up a consolatory prayer for all mankind. In truth, there was no enemy for whom he did not intercede. He prayed for his gaolers, for his executioner, for the Ordinary, for his wife, for Mrs. Thompson, his drunken doxy, and he went to his death with the sure step of one who, having done his duty, is reconciled with the world. The mob testified its affectionate admiration by dubbing him u Charley," and remembered with effusion his last grim pleasantry. "What is the scaffold"? he asked with sublime earnestness. And the answer came quick and sanctimonious: "A short cut to Heaven"!

III
A PARALLEL

(DEACON BRODIE AND CHARLES PEACE)

NOT a parallel, but a contrast, since at all points Peace is Brodie's antithesis.

The one is the austerest of Classics, caring only for the ultimate perfection of his work. The other is the gayest of Romantics, happiest when by the way he produces a glittering effect, or dazzles the ear by a vain impertinence. Now, it is by thievery that Peace reached magnificence. A natural aptitude drove him from the fiddle to the centre-bit. He did but rob, because genius followed the impulse. He had studied the remotest details of his business; he was sternly professional in the conduct of his life, and, as became an old gaol-bird, there was no antic of the policeman wherewith he was not familiar. Moreover, not only had he reduced housebreaking to a science, but, being ostensibly nothing better than a picture-frame maker, he had invented an incomparable set of tools wherewith to enter and evade his neighbour's house. Brodie, on the other hand, was a thief for distraction. His method was as slovenly as ignorance could make it. Though by trade a wright, and therefore a master of all the arts of joinery, he was so deficient in seriousness that he stole a coulter wherewith to batter the walls of the Excise Office. While Peace fought the battle in solitude, Brodie was not only attended by a gang, but listened to the command of his subordinates, and was never permitted-to perform a more intricate duty than the sounding of the alarm. And yet here is the ironical contrast. Peace, the professional thief, despised his brothers, and was never heard to patter a word of flash. Brodie, the amateur, courted the society of all cross-coves, and would rather express himself in Pedlar's French than in his choicest Scots. While the Englishman scraped Tate and Brady from a one-stringed fiddle, the Scot limped a chaunt from *The Beggar's Opera,* and thought himself a devil of a fellow. The one was a man about town masquerading as a thief; the other the most serious among housebreakers, singing psalms in all good faith.

But if Peace was incomparably the better craftsman, Brodie was the prettier gentleman. Peace would not have permitted Brodie to drive his pony-trap the length of Evelina Road. But Brodie, in revenge, would have cut Peace had he met him in the Corn-market. The one was a sombre savage, the other a jovial comrade, and it was a witty freak of fortune that impelled both to follow the same trade. And thus you arrive at another point of difference. The Englishman had no intelligence of life's amenity. He knew naught of costume: clothes were the limit of his ambition. Dressed always for work, he was like the caterpillar which assumes the green of the leaf, wherein it hides: he wore only such duds as should attract the smallest notice, and separate him as far as might be from his business. But the Scot was as fine a dandy as ever took (haphazard) to the cracking of kens. If his refinement permitted no excess of splendour, he went ever gloriously and appropriately apparelled. He was well-mannered, cultured, with scarce a touch of provincialism to mar his gay demeanour: whereas Peace knew little enough outside the practice of burglary, and the proper handling of the revolver.

Our Charles, for example, could neither spell nor write; he dissembled his low origin with the utmost difficulty, and at the best was plastered over (when not at work) with the parochialism of the suburbs. So far the contrast is complete; and even in their similarities there is an evident difference. Each led a double life; but while Brodie was most himself among his own kind, the real Peace was to be found not fiddle-scraping in Evelina Road but marking down policemen in the dusky by-ways of Blackheath. Brodie's grandeur was natural to him; Peace's respectability, so far as it transcended the man's origin, was a cloak of villainy.

Each, again, was an inventor, and while the more innocent Brodie designed a gallows, the more hardened Peace would have gained notoriety by the raising of wrecks and the patronage of Mr. Plimsoll. And since both preserved a certain courage to the end, since both died on the scaffold as becomes a man, the contrast is once more characteristic. Brodie's cynicism is a fine foil to the piety of Peace; and while each end was natural after its own fashion, there is none who will deny to the Scot the finer sense of fitness. Nor did any step in their career explain more clearly the difference in their temperament than their definitions of the gallows. For Peace it is u a short cut to Heaven"; for Brodie it is "a leap in the dark." Again the Scot has the advantage. Again you reflect that, if Peace is the most accomplished Classic among the housebreakers, the Deacon is the merriest companion who ever climbed the gallows by the shoulders of the incomparable Macheath.

THE MAN IN THE GREY SUIT

THE Abbé Bruneau, who gave his shaven head in atonement for unnumbered crimes, was a finished exponent of duplicity. In the eye of day and of Entrammes he shone a miracle of well-doing; by night he prowled in the secret places of Laval.

The world watched him, habited in the decent black of his calling; no sooner was he beyond sight of his parish than his valise was opened, and he arrayed himself— under the hedge, no doubt—in a suit of jaunty grey. The pleasures for which he sacrificed the lives of others and his own were squalid enough, but they were the best a provincial brain might imagine; and he sinned the sins of a hedge priest with a courage and effrontery which his brethren may well envy. Indeed, the Man in the Grey Suit will be sent down the ages with a grimmer scandal, if with a staler mystery, than the Man in the Iron Mask.

He was born of parents who were certainly poor, and possibly honest, at Assé-le-Berenger. He counted a dozen Chouans among his ancestry, and brigandage swam in his blood. Even his childhood was crimson with crimes, which the quick memory of the country-side long ago lost in the pride of having bred a priest. He stained his first cure of souls with the poor, sad sin of arson, which the bishop, fearful of scandal and loth to check a promising career, condoned with a suitable advancement. At Entrammes, his next benefice, he entered into his full inheritance of villainy, and here it was—despite his own protest—that he devised the grey suit which brought him ruin and immortality. To the wild, hilarious dissipation of Laval, the nearest town, he fell an immediate and unresisting prey. Think of the glittering lamps, the sparkling taverns, the bright-eyed women, the manifold fascinations, which are the character and delight of this forgotten city! Why, if the Abbé Bruneau doled out comfort and absolution at Entrammes—why should he not enjoy at Laval the wilder joys of the flesh? Lack of money was the only hindrance, since our priest was not of those who could pursue *bonnes fortunes;* ever he sighed for "booze and the blowens," but "booze and the blowens" he could only purchase with the sovereigns his honest calling denied him. There was no resource but thievery and embezzlement, sins which led sometimes to falsehood or incendiarism, and at a pinch to the graver enterprise of murder. But Bruneau was not one to boggle at trifles. Women he would encounter—young or old, dark or fair, ugly or beautiful, it was all one to him—and the fools who withheld him riches must be punished for their niggard hand. For a while a theft here and there, a cunning extortion of money upon the promise of good works, sufficed for his necessities, but still he hungered for a coup, and patiently he devised and watched his opportunity.

Meanwhile his cunning protected him, and even if the gaze of suspicion fell upon him he contrived his orgies with so neat a discretion that the Church, which is not wont to expose her malefactors, preserved a timid and an innocent silence. The Abbé disappeared with a commendable constancy, and with that just sense of secrecy which should compel even an archiepiscopal admiration. He was not of those who would drag his cloth through the mire. Not until the darkness he loved so fervently covered the earth would he escape from the dull respectability of Entrammes, nor did he ever thus escape unaccompanied by his famous valise. The grey suit was an effectual disguise to his calling, and so jealous was he of the Church's honour that he never—unless in his cups—disclosed his tonsure. One of his innumerable loves confessed in the witness-box that Bruneau always retained his hat in the glare of the cafe, protesting that a headache rendered him fatally susceptible to draught; and such was his thoughtful punctilio that even in the comparative solitude of a guilty bed-chamber he covered his shorn locks with a nightcap.

And while his conduct at Laval was unimpeachable, he always proved a nice susceptibility in his return. A cab carried him within a discreet distance of his home, whence, having exchanged the grey for the more sober black, he would tramp on foot, and thus creep in tranquil and unobserved. But simple as it is to enjoy, enjoyment must still be purchased, and the Abbé was never guilty of a meanness. The less guilty scheme was speedily staled, and then it was that the Abbé bethought him of murder.

His first victim was the widow Bourdais, who pursued the honest calling of a florist at Laval. Already the curate was on those terms of intimacy which unite the robber with the robbed; for some months earlier he had imposed a forced loan of sixty francs upon his victim. But on the 15th of July 1893, he left Entrammes, resolved upon a serious measure. The black valise was in his hand, as he set forth upon the arid, windy road. Before he reached Laval he had made the accustomed transformation, and it was no priest, but a layman, doucely habited in grey, that awaited Mme. Bourdais' return from the flower-market. He entered the shop with the coolness of a friend, and retreated to the door of the parlour when two girls came to make a purchase. No sooner had the widow joined him than he cut her throat, and, with the ferocity of the beast who loves blood as well as plunder, inflicted some forty wounds upon her withered frame. His escape was simple and dignified; he called the cabman, who knew him well, and who knew, moreover, what was required of him; and the priest was snugly in bed, though perhaps exhausted with blood and pleasure, when the news of the murder followed him to his village.

Next day the crime was common gossip, and the Abbé's friends took counsel with him. One there was astonished that the culprit remained undiscovered. "But why should you marvel?" said Bruneau. "I could kill you and your wife at your own chimney-corner without a soul knowing. Had I taken to evil courses instead of to good I should have been a terrible assassin." There is a touch of the pride which De Quincey attributes to Williams in this boastfulness, and throughout the parallel is irresistible. Williams, however, was the better dandy; he put on a dress-coat and patent-leather pumps because the dignity of his work demanded a fitting costume. And Bruneau wore the grey suit not without a hope of disguise. But yet you like to think that the Abbé looked complacently upon his valise, and had forethought for the cut of his professional coat; and if he be not in the first flight of artistry, remember his provincial upbringing, and furnish the proper excuse.

Meanwhile, the scandal of the murdered widow passed into forgetfulness, and the Abbé was still impoverished. Already he had robbed his vicar, and the suspicion of the Abbé Fricot led on to the final and the detected crime. Now Fricot had noted the loss of money and of bonds, and though he refrained from exposure he had confessed to a knowledge of the criminal. M. Bruneau was naturally sensitive to suspicion, and he determined upon the immediate removal of this danger to his peace. On January 2, 1894, M. Fricot returned to supper after administering the extreme unction to a parishioner. While the meal was preparing, he went into his garden in sabots and bareheaded, and never again was seen alive. The supper cooled, the vicar was still absent; the murderer, hungry with his toil, ate not only his own, but his victim's share of the food, grimly hinting that Fricot would not come back. Suicide was dreamed of, murder hinted; up and down the village was the search made, and none was more zealous than the distressed curate.

At last a peasant discovered some blocks of wood in the well, and before long blood-stains revealed themselves on the masonry. Speedily was the body recovered, disfigured and battered beyond recognition, and the voice of the village went up in denunciation of the Abbé Bruneau. Immunity had made the culprit callous, and in a few hours suspicion became certainty. A bleeding nose was the lame explanation given for the stains which were on his clothes, on the table, on the keys of his harmonium. A quaint and characteristic folly was it that drove the murderer straight to the solace of his religion. You picture him, hot and red-handed from murder, soothing his battered conscience with some devilish *Requiem* for the unshrived soul he had just parted from its broken body, and leaving upon the harmonium the ineradicable traces of his guilt. Thus he lived, poised between murder and the Church, spending upon the vulgar dissipation of a Breton village the blood and money of his foolish victims. But for him "les tavernes et les filles" of Laval meant a veritable paradise, and his sojourn in the country is proof enough of a limited cunning. Had he been more richly endowed, Paris had been the theatre of his crimes. As it is, he goes down to posterity as the Man in the Grey Suit, and the best friend the cabmen of Laval ever knew. Them, indeed, he left inconsolable.

MONSIEUR L'ABBÉ

THE childhood of the Abbé Rosselot is as secret as his origin, and no man may know whether Belfort or Bavaria smiled upon his innocence. A like mystery enshrouds his early manhood, and the malice of his foes, who are legion, denounces him for a Jesuit of Innsbruck. But since he has lived within the eye of the world his villainies have been revealed as clearly as his attainments, and history provides him no other rival in the corruption of youth than the infamous Thwackum.

It is not every scholar's ambition to teach the elements, and Rosselot adopted his modest calling as a cloak of crime. No sooner was he installed in a mansion than he became the mansion's master, and henceforth he ruled his employer's domain with the tyrannical severity of a Grand Inquisitor. His soul wrapped in the triple brass of arrogance, he even dared to lay his hands upon food before his betters were served; and presently, emboldened by success, he would order the dinners, reproach the cook with a too lavish use of condiments, and descend with insolent expostulation into the kitchen. In a week he had opened the cupboards upon a dozen skeletons, and made them rattle their rickety bones up and down the draughty staircases, until the inmates shivered with horror and the terrified neighbours fled the haunted mansion as a lazar-house. Once in possession of a family secret, he felt himself secure, and henceforth he was free to browbeat his employer and to flog his pupil to the satisfaction of his waspish nature. Moreover, he was endowed with all the insight and effrontery of a trained interviewer. So sedulous was he in his search after the truth, that neither man nor woman could deny him confidence. And, as vinegar flowed in his veins for blood, it was his merry sport to set wife against husband and children against father. Not even were the servants safe from his watchful inquiry, and housemaids and governesses alike entrusted their hopes and fears to his malicious keeping. And when the house had retired to rest, with what a sinister delight did he chuckle over the frailties and infamies, a guilty knowledge of which he had dragged from many an unwilling sinner! To oust him, when installed, was a plain impossibility, for this wringer of hearts was only too glib in the surrender of another's scandal; and as he accepted the last scurrility with Christian resignation, his unfortunate employer could but strengthen his vocabulary and patiently endure the presence of this smiling, demoniacal tutor.

But a too villainous curiosity was not the Abbé's capital sin. Not only did he entertain his leisure with wrecking the happiness of a united family, but he was an enemy open and declared of France. It was his amiable pastime at the dinner-table, when he had first helped himself to such delicacies as tempted his dainty palate, to pronounce a pompous eulogy upon the German Emperor. France, he would say with an exultant smile, is a ***pays pourri,*** which exists merely to be the football of Prussia. She has but one hope of salvation—still the monster speaks—and that is to fall into the benign occupation of a vigorous race. Once upon a time—the infamy is scarce credible—he was conducting his young charges past a town-hall, over the lintel of whose door glittered those proud initials "R. F." "What do they stand for?" asked this demon Barlow. And when the patriotic Tommy hesitated for an answer, the preceptor exclaimed with ineffable contempt, "Race de fous"! It is no wonder, then, that this foe of his fatherland feared to receive a letter openly addressed; rather he would slink out under cover of night and seek his correspondence at the ***poste restante,*** like a guilty lover or a British tourist.

The Château de Presles was built for his reception. It was haunted by a secret, which none dare murmur in the remotest garret. There was no more than a whisper of murder in the air, but the Marquis shuddered when his wife's eye frowned upon him. True, the miserable Menaldo had disappeared from his seminary ten years since, but threats of disclosure were uttered continually, and respectability might only be purchased by a profound silence. Here was the Abbé's most splendid opportunity, and he seized it with all the eagerness of a greedy temperament. The Marquise, a wealthy peasant, who was rather at home on the wild hill-side than in her stately castle, became an instant prey to his devilish intrigue. The governess, an antic old maid of fifty-seven, whose conversation was designed to bring a blush to the cheek of the most hardened dragoon, was immediately on terms of so frank an intimacy that she flung bread pellets at him across the table, and joyously proposed, if we may believe the priest on his oath, to set up housekeeping with him, that they might save expense. Two high-spirited boys were always at hand to encourage his taste for flogging, and had it not been for the Marquis, the Abbé's cup would have been full to overflowing. But the Marquis loved not the lean, ogling instructor of his sons, and presently began to assail him with all the abuse of which he was master. He charged the Abbé with unspeakable villainy; *salop* and *saligaud* were the terms in which he would habitually refer to him. He knew the rascal for a spy, and no modesty restrained him from proclaiming his knowledge. But whatever insults were thrown at the Abbé he received with a grin complacent as Shy-lock's, for was he not conscious that when he liked the pound of flesh was his own!

With a fiend's duplicity he laid his plans of ruin and death. The Marquise, swayed to his will, received him secretly in the blue room (whose very colour suggests a guilty intrigue), though never, upon the oath of an Abbé, when the key was turned in the lock. A journey to Switzerland had freed him from the haunting suspicion of the Marquis, and at last he might compel the wife to denounce her husband as a murderer. The terrified woman drew the indictment at the Abbé's dictation, and when her husband returned to St. Amand he was instantly thrust into prison. Nothing remained but to cajole the sons into an expressed hatred of their father, and the last enormity was committed by a masterpiece of cunning. "Your father's one chance of escape," argued this villain in a cassock, "is to be proved an inhuman ruffian. Swear that he beat you unmercifully and you will save him from the guillotine." All the dupes learned their lesson with a certainty which reflects infinite credit upon the Abbé's method of instruction.

For once in his life the Abbé had been moved by greed as well as by villainy. His early exploits had no worse motive than the satisfaction of an inhuman lust for cruelty and destruction. But the Marquise was rich, and once her husband's head were off, might not the Abbé reap his share of the gathered harvest? The stakes were high, but the game was worth the playing, and Rosselot played it with spirit and energy unto the last card. His appearance in court is ever memorable, and as his ferret eyes glinted through glass at the President, he seemed the villain of some Middle Age Romance. His head, poised upon a lean, bony frame, was embellished with a nose thin and sharp as the blade of a knife; his tightly compressed lips were an indication of the rascal's determination. "Long as a day in Lent"—that is how a spectator described him; and if ever a sinister nature glared through a sinister figure, the Abbé's character was revealed before he parted his lips in speech. Unmoved he stood and immovable; he treated the imprecations of the Marquis with a cold disdain; as the burden of proof grew heavy on his back, he shrugged his shoulders in weary indifference. He told his monstrous story with a cynical contempt, which has scarce its equal in the history of crime; and priest, as he was, he proved that he did not yield to the Marquis himself in the Rabelaisian amplitude of his vocabulary. He brought charges against the weird world of Presles with an insouciance and brutality which defeated their own aim. He described the vices of his master and the sins of the servants in a slang which would sit more gracefully upon an idle roysterer than upon a pious Abbé. And, his story ended, he leered at the Court with the satisfaction of one who had discharged a fearsome duty.

But his rascality overshot its mark; the Marquise, obedient to his priestly casuistry, displayed too fierce a zeal in the execution of his commands. And he took to flight, hoping to lose in the larger world of Paris the notoriety which his prowess won him among the poor despised Berrichons. He left behind for our consolation a snatch of philosophy which helps to explain his last and greatest achievement. "Those who have money exist only to be fleeced." Thus he spake, with a reckless revelation of self. Yet the mystery of his being is still unpierced. He is traitor, schemer, spy; but is he an Abbé? Perhaps not. At any rate, he once attended the "Messe des Morts," and was heard to mumble a "Credo," which, as every good Catholic remembers, has no place in that solemn service.

www.bookjungle.com *email: sales@bookjungle.com fax: 630-214-0564 mail: Book Jungle PO Box 2226 Champaign, IL 61825*

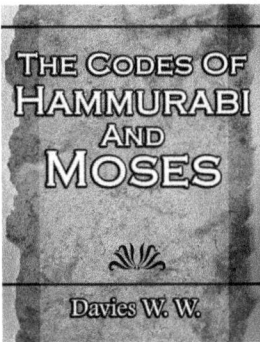

The Codes Of Hammurabi And Moses
W. W. Davies

QTY

The discovery of the Hammurabi Code is one of the greatest achievements of archaeology, and is of paramount interest, not only to the student of the Bible, but also to all those interested in ancient history...

Religion   **ISBN:** *1-59462-338-4*   **Pages:132**
MSRP $12.95

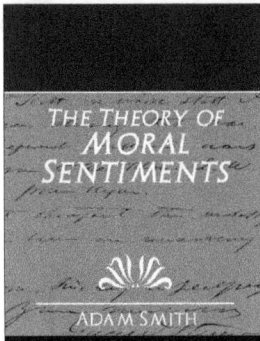

The Theory of Moral Sentiments
Adam Smith

QTY

This work from 1749. contains original theories of conscience amd moral judgment and it is the foundation for systemof morals.

Philosophy **ISBN:** *1-59462-777-0*   **Pages:536**
MSRP $19.95

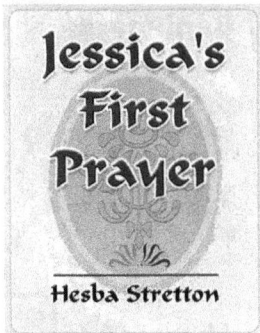

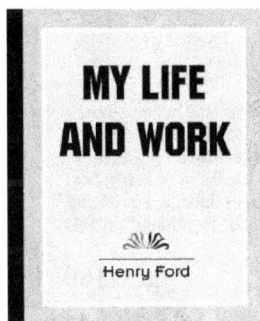

Jessica's First Prayer
Hesba Stretton

QTY

In a screened and secluded corner of one of the many railway-bridges which span the streets of London there could be seen a few years ago, from five o'clock every morning until half past eight, a tidily set-out coffee-stall, consisting of a trestle and board, upon which stood two large tin cans, with a small fire of charcoal burning under each so as to keep the coffee boiling during the early hours of the morning when the work-people were thronging into the city on their way to their daily toil...

Pages:84

Childrens   **ISBN:** *1-59462-373-2*   *MSRP $9.95*

My Life and Work
Henry Ford

QTY

Henry Ford revolutionized the world with his implementation of mass production for the Model T automobile. Gain valuable business insight into his life and work with his own auto-biography... "We have only started on our development of our country we have not as yet, with all our talk of wonderful progress, done more than scratch the surface. The progress has been wonderful enough but..."

Pages:300

Biographies/   **ISBN:** *1-59462-198-5*   *MSRP $21.95*

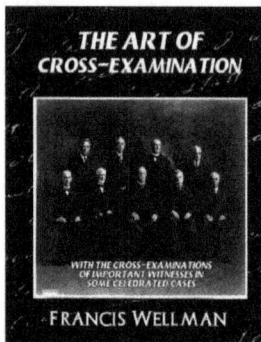

The Art of Cross-Examination
Francis Wellman

QTY

I presume it is the experience of every author, after his first book is published upon an important subject, to be almost overwhelmed with a wealth of ideas and illustrations which could readily have been included in his book, and which to his own mind, at least, seem to make a second edition inevitable. Such certainly was the case with me; and when the first edition had reached its sixth impression in five months, I rejoiced to learn that it seemed to my publishers that the book had met with a sufficiently favorable reception to justify a second and considerably enlarged edition. ..

Pages:412

Reference   ISBN: *1-59462-647-2*   *MSRP $19.95*

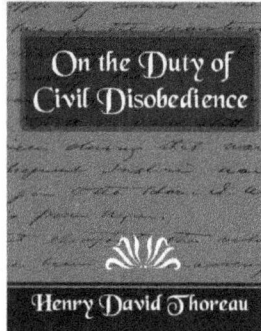

On the Duty of Civil Disobedience
Henry David Thoreau

QTY

Thoreau wrote his famous essay, On the Duty of Civil Disobedience, as a protest against an unjust but popular war and the immoral but popular institution of slave-owning. He did more than write—he declined to pay his taxes, and was hauled off to gaol in consequence. Who can say how much this refusal of his hastened the end of the war and of slavery ?

Law   ISBN: *1-59462-747-9*   **Pages:48**

MSRP $7.45

Dream Psychology Psychoanalysis for Beginners
Sigmund Freud

QTY

Sigmund Freud, born Sigismund Schlomo Freud (May 6, 1856 - September 23, 1939), was a Jewish-Austrian neurologist and psychiatrist who co-founded the psychoanalytic school of psychology. Freud is best known for his theories of the unconscious mind, especially involving the mechanism of repression; his redefinition of sexual desire as mobile and directed towards a wide variety of objects; and his therapeutic techniques, especially his understanding of transference in the therapeutic relationship and the presumed value of dreams as sources of insight into unconscious desires.

Pages:196

Psychology   ISBN: *1-59462-905-6*   *MSRP $15.45*

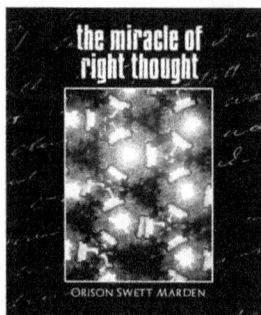

The Miracle of Right Thought
Orison Swett Marden

QTY

Believe with all of your heart that you will do what you were made to do. When the mind has once formed the habit of holding cheerful, happy, prosperous pictures, it will not be easy to form the opposite habit. It does not matter how improbable or how far away this realization may see, or how dark the prospects may be, if we visualize them as best we can, as vividly as possible, hold tenaciously to them and vigorously struggle to attain them, they will gradually become actualized, realized in the life. But a desire, a longing without endeavor, a yearning abandoned or held indifferently will vanish without realization.

Pages:360

Self Help   ISBN: *1-59462-644-8*   *MSRP $25.45*

QTY

The Rosicrucian Cosmo-Conception Mystic Christianity *by Max Heindel* ISBN: *1-59462-188-8* **$38.95**
The Rosicrucian Cosmo-conception is not dogmatic, neither does it appeal to any other authority than the reason of the student. It is: not controversial, but is: sent forth in the, hope that it may help to clear... New Age/Religion Pages 646

Abandonment To Divine Providence *by Jean-Pierre de Caussade* ISBN: *1-59462-228-0* **$25.95**
"The Rev. Jean Pierre de Caussade was one of the most remarkable spiritual writers of the Society of Jesus in France in the 18th Century. His death took place at Toulouse in 1751. His works have gone through many editions and have been republished... Inspirational/Religion Pages 400

Mental Chemistry *by Charles Haanel* ISBN: *1-59462-192-6* **$23.95**
Mental Chemistry allows the change of material conditions by combining and appropriately utilizing the power of the mind. Much like applied chemistry creates something new and unique out of careful combinations of chemicals the mastery of mental chemistry... New Age Pages 354

The Letters of Robert Browning and Elizabeth Barret Barrett 1845-1846 vol II ISBN: *1-59462-193-4* **$35.95**
by Robert Browning and Elizabeth Barrett Biographies Pages 596

Gleanings In Genesis (volume I) *by Arthur W. Pink* ISBN: *1-59462-130-6* **$27.45**
Appropriately has Genesis been termed "the seed plot of the Bible" for in it we have, in germ form, almost all of the great doctrines which are afterwards fully developed in the books of Scripture which follow... Religion/Inspirational Pages 420

The Master Key *by L. W. de Laurence* ISBN: *1-59462-001-6* **$30.95**
In no branch of human knowledge has there been a more lively increase of the spirit of research during the past few years than in the study of Psychology, Concentration and Mental Discipline. The requests for authentic lessons in Thought Control, Mental Discipline and... New Age/Psychology Pages 422

The Lesser Key Of Solomon Goetia *by L. W. de Laurence* ISBN: *1-59462-092-X* **$9.95**
This translation of the first book of the "Lernegton" which is now for the first time made accessible to students of Talismanic Magic was done, after careful collation and edition, from numerous Ancient Manuscripts in Hebrew, Latin, and French... New Age/Occult Pages 92

Rubaiyat Of Omar Khayyam *by Edward Fitzgerald* ISBN: *1-59462-332-5* **$13.95**
Edward Fitzgerald, whom the world has already learned, in spite of his own efforts to remain within the shadow of anonymity, to look upon as one of the rarest poets of the century, was born at Bredfield, in Suffolk, on the 31st of March, 1809. He was the third son of John Purcell... Music Pages 172

Ancient Law *by Henry Maine* ISBN: *1-59462-128-4* **$29.95**
The chief object of the following pages is to indicate some of the earliest ideas of mankind, as they are reflected in Ancient Law, and to point out the relation of those ideas to modern thought. Religion/History Pages 452

Far-Away Stories *by William J. Locke* ISBN: *1-59462-129-2* **$19.45**
"Good wine needs no bush, but a collection of mixed vintages does. And this book is just such a collection. Some of the stories I do not want to remain buried for ever in the museum files of dead magazine-numbers an author's not unpardonable vanity..." Fiction Pages 272

Life of David Crockett *by David Crockett* ISBN: *1-59462-250-7* **$27.45**
"Colonel David Crockett was one of the most remarkable men of the times in which he lived. Born in humble life, but gifted with a strong will, an indomitable courage, and unremitting perseverance... Biographies/New Age Pages 424

Lip-Reading *by Edward Nitchie* ISBN: *1-59462-206-X* **$25.95**
Edward B. Nitchie, founder of the New York School for the Hard of Hearing, now the Nitchie School of Lip-Reading, Inc, wrote "LIP-READING Principles and Practice". The development and perfecting of this meritorious work on lip-reading was an undertaking... How-to Pages 400

A Handbook of Suggestive Therapeutics, Applied Hypnotism, Psychic Science ISBN: *1-59462-214-0* **$24.95**
by Henry Munro Health/New Age/Health/Self-help Pages 376

A Doll's House: and Two Other Plays *by Henrik Ibsen* ISBN: *1-59462-112-8* **$19.95**
Henrik Ibsen created this classic when in revolutionary 1848 Rome. Introducing some striking concepts in playwriting for the realist genre, this play has been studied the world over. Fiction/Classics/Plays 308

The Light of Asia *by sir Edwin Arnold* ISBN: *1-59462-204-3* **$13.95**
In this poetic masterpiece, Edwin Arnold describes the life and teachings of Buddha. The man who was to become known as Buddha to the world was born as Prince Gautama of India but he rejected the worldly riches and abandoned the reigns of power when... Religion/History/Biographies Pages 170

The Complete Works of Guy de Maupassant *by Guy de Maupassant* ISBN: *1-59462-157-8* **$16.95**
"For days and days, nights and nights, I had dreamed of that first kiss which was to consecrate our engagement, and I knew not on what spot I should put my lips..." Fiction/Classics Pages 240

The Art of Cross-Examination *by Francis L. Wellman* ISBN: *1-59462-309-0* **$26.95**
Written by a renowned trial lawyer, Wellman imparts his experience and uses case studies to explain how to use psychology to extract desired information through questioning. How-to/Science/Reference Pages 408

Answered or Unanswered? *by Louisa Vaughan* ISBN: *1-59462-248-5* **$10.95**
Miracles of Faith in China Religion Pages 112

The Edinburgh Lectures on Mental Science (1909) *by Thomas* ISBN: *1-59462-008-3* **$11.95**
This book contains the substance of a course of lectures recently given by the writer in the Queen Street Hail, Edinburgh. Its purpose is to indicate the Natural Principles governing the relation between Mental Action and Material Conditions... New Age/Psychology Pages 148

Ayesha *by H. Rider Haggard* ISBN: *1-59462-301-5* **$24.95**
Verily and indeed it is the unexpected that happens! Probably if there was one person upon the earth from whom the Editor of this, and of a certain previous history, did not expect to hear again... Classics Pages 380

Ayala's Angel *by Anthony Trollope* ISBN: *1-59462-352-X* **$29.95**
The two girls were both pretty, but Lucy who was twenty-one who supposed to be simple and comparatively unattractive, whereas Ayala was credited, as her Bombwhat romantic name might show, with poetic charm and a taste for romance. Ayala when her father died was nineteen... Fiction Pages 484

The American Commonwealth *by James Bryce* ISBN: *1-59462-286-8* **$34.45**
An interpretation of American democratic political theory. It examines political mechanics and society from the perspective of Scotsman James Bryce Politics Pages 572

Stories of the Pilgrims *by Margaret P. Pumphrey* ISBN: *1-59462-116-0* **$17.95**
This book explores pilgrims religious oppression in England as well as their escape to Holland and eventual crossing to America on the Mayflower, and their early days in New England... History Pages 268

www.ingramcontent.com/pod-product-compliance
Lightning Source LLC
Chambersburg PA
CBHW081232090426

42738CB00016B/3261